Instant Pot Korean Cookbook

INSTANT POT
KOREAN
COOKBOOK

Traditional Favorites Made Fast and Easy

Christy Lee

Photography by Elysa Weitala

ROCKRIDGE
PRESS

Interior and Cover Designer: Stephanie Mautone
Art Producer: Sue Bischofberger
Editor: Cecily McAndrews
Production Editor: Ashley Polikoff
Production Manager: Martin Worthington

Photography © 2022 Elysa Weitala. Food styling by Victoria Woollard.
Cover: Jangjorim (Soy-Braised Beef with Eggs), page 86

Paperback ISBN: 978-1-638-07851-7
Ebook ISBN: 978-1-638-07607-0
R0

*For my beautiful Sora,
who is always up late,
keeping the closet
monsters away while
watching me experiment
in the kitchen.*

CONTENTS

INTRODUCTION viii

1 The Korean Kitchen 1

2 Appetizers and Sides 17

3 Soups and Stews 35

4 Vegetable Dishes 57

5 Beef and Pork Dishes 73

6 Poultry and Seafood Dishes 99

MEASUREMENT CONVERSIONS 119

RESOURCES 120

INSTANT POT COOKING CHARTS 121

INDEX 127

INTRODUCTION

Welcome to the world of Korean Instant Pot cooking. As a trained chef and food enthusiast, it's my pleasure to introduce you to a fast, easy way to make delicious Korean food at home. Although I appreciate a wide range of different cuisines, my original love is Korean food; in fact, I currently sell Korean meals to local customers as part of a home-cooked meal delivery service that connects local cooks with clients in their communities. My dishes are freshly cooked and prepared using family recipes, and they get delivered to customers in nearby cities.

Growing up in a Korean household, I always had healthy, delicious, home-cooked food prepared by my mom and grandma, who also happen to be my greatest mentors in the kitchen. I remember waking up every morning and coming down to the kitchen to see my grandmother standing over the stove. She'd start soup at 6 in the morning for us to enjoy for breakfast, because so many traditional recipes required long cooking. They used the freshest ingredients to prepare the entire spectrum of flavorful Korean dishes while teaching me how to create these complex, timeless recipes. The time, dedication, and love that went into their cooking did not go unnoticed, but few cooks today have that kind of time, no matter how much they love their families.

Enter the Instant Pot. My first experience with this game-changing piece of equipment was back in 2016, when I received one as a Christmas gift from a friend. Not knowing anything about this device, I was intimidated at first and wasn't sure if I'd ever use it. It sat in the corner for a couple of months until I took a chance, opened the box, and made my very first recipe, Kkori Gomtang, or Korean Oxtail Soup (page 48). Traditionally, it would take more than five hours to cook this soup on the stovetop, but with the touch of a button, it was ready in just an hour. And it was perfect, with super-tender meat and deeply flavored, silky broth.

After that initial success, I began experimenting with other recipes and tried the Instant Pot for everything that would normally require long hours of simmering or braising on the stove. To my delight, I found that most dishes were ready in less than 90 minutes. Eventually, I started using the Instant Pot for less obvious dishes, including Korean rice cakes, porridge, and even punch drinks. After getting quite comfortable with it, I tried the pot-in-pot method, so that I can cook two things at once, such as the Ground Beef Bulgogi with Rice (page 88), where the rice steams in a bowl on the trivet while the beef mixture simmers below. And a serious bonus? Fewer dishes and easier cleanup.

Weekdays are the hardest times for most people to cook, when many of us come home from work late, tired and hungry. Everyone seems to want quick recipes. That is part of what I am here for. I've developed recipes for numerous Korean dishes that require very little prep and cooking time in the Instant Pot. Although a typical Korean meal can take many hours to make, some soups in this book—like the Gamja Guk, or Egg Drop Potato Soup (page 42), or Seogogi Mu Guk, or Daikon Soup (page 36)—can be made in about 30 minutes while you cook the rice. It will open up worlds of hearty meals that you can prepare with relative ease and speed without sacrificing health or deliciousness.

It's my distinct pleasure to help bring these traditional meals to your table in an accessible way. Every recipe in this book lets you cook authentic Korean dishes using ingredients you can easily find at your local Korean market or online. As I developed the recipes, I relied on the feedback of my audience on YouTube (Christy's Kitchen) and Instagram (@Christy_L_Kitchen), so you can be sure the recipes are thoroughly tested, critiqued, and foolproof. I hope you will enjoy the range of dishes offered here from my kitchen to your table. Happy cooking!

1

The Korean Kitchen

THIS CHAPTER WILL DISCUSS ALL THE WAYS THE INSTANT POT CAN BE USED FOR CREATING DELICIOUS KOREAN MEALS. It will explain how to sauté, steam, braise, stew, and simmer. You'll learn the basics of cooking rice and noodles in the Instant Pot. And the chapter will delve into the fundamentals of building complex flavors in Korean cooking using spices, herbs, and condiments, along with an explanation of how to alter the spiciness of a recipe to suit your own tastes. Finally, this chapter will provide you with an overview of the basic fresh ingredients and pantry staples that commonly appear in the recipes.

Korean Cooking and the Instant Pot

This versatile multi-cooker is practically a Korean kitchen in itself. The Instant Pot allows users to perform a variety of cooking methods, all of which make it easy to prepare dozens of Korean dishes in a fraction of the time they traditionally take. From broth and soup to side dishes, rice, and main dishes, the Instant Pot can make them all. Here's a rundown of the cooking methods you'll use in this book's recipes.

Sautéing to Build Flavor

Some recipes ask that you begin by sautéing some of the ingredients before pressure cooking. In others, you'll use the Sauté function to finish sauces after pressure cooking. The Sauté function has three heat levels: Low, Medium, or High (on some models of the Instant Pot, the levels are Less, Normal, and More). Generally, you'll use Low (Less) for thickening sauces or simmering soups. Medium (Normal) is best for sautéing vegetables. Use High (More) to brown or sear meat. The Sauté function automatically turns off after 30 minutes, although you can increase or decrease the time if you like. You can also simply cancel the function when you're done cooking.

To sauté, select the Sauté function, and adjust the heat to the desired level. Let the pot heat up with oil. When the display reads "Hot," add the ingredients to be sautéed and cook as directed. When done, press the Cancel or Off button. You may then finish the cooking process by switching to the pressure-cooking function.

Steaming

The Instant Pot is great for pressure-steaming vegetables, fish, pork ribs, chicken, rice cakes, dumplings, and frozen foods. Depending on what you're steaming, most foods will be ready in less than 3 minutes, plus the time to build pressure.

The Instant Pot comes with a metal trivet that fits in the inner pot. Bulky vegetables, such as corn or sweet potatoes, can be placed directly on top of the trivet to steam. Most vegetables will need to be placed inside a bowl or a steamer basket, however. Steamer baskets are available in silicone, bamboo, and metal (either mesh baskets or collapsible steamers). For dumplings, I like to use a bamboo steamer with a lid. For some vegetables, it's worth investing in a "pot-in-pot" insert that you can stack so you can cook two dishes at once. You can stack a set of aluminum pans on top of each other, each holding a different type of vegetable.

To pressure steam, start by adding water to the pot, usually 1 cup. Place your steamer insert inside the inner pot, and add the ingredients to be steamed. Lock the Instant Pot lid into place, making sure to seal the vent. You can steam using either the Steam function or the Pressure Cook (Manual) function. The Steam function heats continuously, whereas the Pressure Cook function cycles on and off, so the Steam function will come to pressure a little faster. In most cases, there's very little difference in results, but if you want to save a minute or so of cooking time, choose Steam. For both functions, you'll adjust the pressure to either Low or High and set the time.

When it comes to most leafy vegetables, I like to cook them on low pressure for 0 minutes and do a quick release. Cooking for 0 minutes might sound strange, but remember that cooking starts as the pot builds pressure, so tender vegetables can be done in just the time it takes it to come up to pressure. Sturdier vegetables, like broccoli, zucchini, and cauliflower, require a steaming basket (which you place directly in the pot) or a heat-safe bowl (which you place on the trivet in the pot) and cooking on High Pressure for 0 to 1 minutes, depending on the thickness of the vegetable.

Small whole fish or fillets can be placed on a plate on top of the trivet. Most shellfish, like shrimp and clams, require a bowl or steamer basket. Because seafood cooks quickly, cook it on low pressure and do a quick release. (Don't overcook seafood, or else it gets rubbery.) I love using the Instant Pot to steam fresh whole crabs, either on the trivet or in a shallow steaming basket. It takes half the time to cook in the Instant Pot versus the stovetop. There's also less smell, and the cleanup is so much easier.

Although the Instant Pot comes with the trivet, you may need to purchase steaming baskets, as well as heat-safe bowls and pots, to place in the Instant Pot. Look for the 6-quart size.

Making Speedy Stocks

The broths and stocks in Korean recipes cook very quickly—less than 10 minutes—in the Instant Pot. Several stocks are used, but most are based on Dashima Myeolchi Yuksu, which directly translates to "dried kelp and dried anchovy broth." Variations include a simple anchovy broth; kelp and mushroom broth; and vegetable broth, which is made from kelp, shiitake mushroom, carrot, daikon, and leeks. I like to enrich the basic stock with dried shrimp, daikon, and dried pollack.

If you plan to cook a lot of Korean dishes, it is a good idea to make a batch of basic anchovy broth (see Kongbiji Jjigae, page 38) ahead to store in the refrigerator.

You can then add flavor-boosting aromatics like garlic, onion, or daikon to this pre-made stock, depending on the dish. This stock is very forgiving, and there is almost no right or wrong ratio between any of the dried seafood ingredients. Broths generally last up to 4 days in the refrigerator and 6 months in the freezer.

The best part is that these ingredients release their unique deep flavors in the Instant Pot very quickly without compromising on taste. In fact, you don't want to cook the dried kelp and dried anchovy stock for too long, or it will become slimy and give off a bad taste.

Braising and Stewing

The Instant Pot offers hands-off, easy cooking when you're braising tough meats. They will cook in just a fraction of the time, and you won't have to wait by the stove. For example, my grandmother's recipe for Kkori Gomtang, or Oxtail Soup (page 48), would normally take more than 4 hours to cook on the stovetop, but using the Instant Pot cuts the cooking time to about 1 hour for this delicious and super traditional comfort food.

To braise, put the meat directly into the pot along with the sauce and aromatics. Set the cooking time, and the Instant Pot does the rest. Most meats can be cooked for 30 to 40 minutes with natural pressure release for super-tender results.

There are a couple of ways you can add more complex flavors to braises and stews. Traditionally, Korean braised meats are not seared, but you can do so by using the Sauté function, as described earlier, for a deeper rich browned-meat flavor. Second, marinating the meat in aromatics overnight can create more depth of flavor in the dish. Simply put all the ingredients in the inner pot, cover it, and let it sit inside the refrigerator overnight. This is a perfect trick to use with Kimchi Jjigae, or Kimchi Stew (page 50). The night before you plan to serve it, add the kimchi, pork, aromatics, and spices to the pot. The next day, place the inner pot in the base of the Instant Pot, lock on the lid, program the cooking process, and you'll soon enjoy a nice bowl of Kimchi Jjigae.

Simmering

Some recipes will require you to add certain ingredients after the pressure-cooking process is over. For instance, when you prepare Tteokguk, or Rice Cake Soup (page 46), you will need to pressure cook the meat first to tenderize and soften it. The rice cake cooks faster and will be added to the soup base last. Simmering can also be used to add last-minute vegetables.

Use the Sauté function to simmer. When adding quick-cooking ingredients like scallions and onions, leafy vegetables like spinach, and herbs, adjust the Sauté mode to Low, and let the broth come to a simmer; slow bubbles will appear on the surface of the broth. Add the ingredients, and cook until they're done. To quickly cook thicker vegetables, adjust the Sauté mode to Medium or High for a rapid boil.

Simmering using the Sauté function also works to thicken sauces by reducing the liquid in the sauce. For some recipes, you may also opt to add a cornstarch and water mixture to the pot after pressure cooking to thicken the sauce. Simply press the Sauté button, adjust to Low heat, and let the liquid come back to a boil. Add the cornstarch mixture, and continue to boil until it thickens.

The Flavors of Korean Cuisine

Korean cuisine is complex, with intense flavors. In addition to the five basic tastes—salty, sour, sweet, bitter, and umami—spiciness is essential to the cuisine. There's a perception that all Korean food is overly spicy. Because the newer generation has embraced spicy food and modern palates are accustomed to it, restaurants have concentrated on fusion-style dishes, adding high levels of spice. But many home cooks prefer a much simpler and cleaner taste, not so spicy but still incredibly flavorful (see Keeping It Spicy, page 7).

Siwonhan-mat

In addition to these six flavors, a unique flavor sensation often mentioned in Korean cuisine is what is called Siwonhan-mat. This term (sometimes translated as "cool") refers to the way some foods feel in the mouth and throat, and further on into the stomach and digestive tract. More than taste or smell, it's a soothing sensation, almost the opposite of indigestion. Soups and stews especially, like Gamja Sujebi, or Umami Hand-Torn Noodles (page 64), have this soothing or refreshing effect when eaten. For instance, when eating a hot chicken soup on a warm summer day, Koreans would compliment the meal by saying it had Siwonhan-mat, meaning that the experience is quite refreshing as the hot soup touches the soft surfaces in their mouth, goes down the throat, and is soothing to digest in the stomach.

This concept of Siwonhan-mat relates back to the historical culture of Korean food and cuisine. Traditionally, Korean food wasn't made purely for taste and presentation as it is today. Cooking was tied into the basic need to survive, so food was viewed in terms of its nutritive and medicinal value. Every ingredient had a purpose to play in safeguarding health, and those properties were the reason various foods were combined. Although this view of cuisine has faded, it's behind many of the dishes still enjoyed today.

Bold and Balanced

Some of the most iconic ingredients elemental to many Korean dishes include fermented red pepper paste, soybean paste, and soy sauce. All three condiments have the same ending of –jang: gochujang, doenjang, and ganjang. The three are all fermented, which contributes an umami taste, and contain an abundance of salt, which acts as a natural preservative. These seasonings are very pungent and can easily overwhelm a dish if used incorrectly.

Although these seasonings play a huge role in Korean cuisine, they're not the only sources of bold flavors. In the Korean kitchen, you'll find that many vegetables are pickled or fermented, stemming from the days when they needed to be preserved to last through the winter. These can either be served on their own or added to dishes to provide umami, saltiness, and acid. Korean dishes also get flavor from garlic, ginger, scallions, sesame oil, and red pepper flakes. And, as mentioned earlier, salted dried fish like anchovies flavor the broth used in many Korean dishes.

In a traditional Korean meal, balance is key. For instance, many stews and casseroles contain tofu because it offsets strong flavors and balances the saltiness and umami of gochujang and fermented vegetables. Milder vegetable dishes, like a seasoned spinach salad, can also balance out bolder flavors. Because most protein is either braised or marinated using the fermented pastes and aromatics, fruits tone down those bold flavors with sweetness. Sugar also creates a nice char on meat when it's grilled and adds another layer of flavor.

Banchan and Kimchi

No Korean meal is complete unless there is seemingly unlimited banchan served at the table. Banchan is the collective name for a number of small side dishes, usually but not always vegetables, served alongside rice, soup, and other main dishes. The more formal the meal, the more banchan served. They're placed in the middle of the table for all to share and replenished as necessary. They can be pickled or fermented like kimchi, braised in a sauce, or steamed and tossed in a dressing. Many of the vegetable banchan dishes originated in Korea's early Buddhist era when meat was not allowed in the temples and vegetables were the focal point of the meal.

Kimchi also plays a large role in the long-standing cultural heritage of Korea. It's served at virtually every meal. Although Americans are most familiar with spicy kimchi made from napa cabbage, there are many types of kimchi made from other vegetables. Some are simply made using a salted brine mixture, whereas others are made with red pepper flakes. The recipe and taste of kimchi varies depending on the region of Korea from which it hails. As you travel to the southern part of Korea, you'll notice that the kimchi has a strong, bold, saltier flavor. When you travel north, the taste is more sour.

Keeping It Spicy

The spice level in Korean food is actually not as high as in some other cuisines. The modern tendency is to use extra levels of spice, but the traditional cooking methods use lower levels. Still, you may find some dishes to be too spicy and have a hard time handling the heat level. When recipes call for either gochujang (fermented red pepper paste) or gochugaru (Korean red chili flakes), you can always adjust the heat level by adding less. When the recipe calls for 1 tablespoon of spice, start with 1 teaspoon. You won't compromise the dish or its flavors when you tone down the spices. You can always add more aromatics like garlic or ginger if you feel the dish needs more flavor. And remember that spicy ingredients are often tempered by adding milder ingredients. For instance, kimchi stew doesn't have to be spicy if you don't add extra gochugaru and chile peppers. Even though the kimchi itself is spicy, the water added to the kimchi will dilute the soup and the spicy flavors. Also, most people can develop a tolerance for spicier food by slowly increasing the spice level of the foods they eat. So you may find that as you try spicier dishes, you come to like them more.

Fried and Stir-Fried Recipes

It doesn't make sense to attempt to fry or stir-fry in the Instant Pot. That is not what it's built for; it can't replicate what a wok can do. Yet that doesn't mean you can't enjoy the flavors of something like Korean fried chicken in a less labor-intensive way. Two great examples are the Jjimdak, or Braised Chicken with Vegetables and Glass Noodles (page 108), or the Maeun Dalknalgae, or Spicy Sticky Chicken Wings (page 114). Cooked in the Instant Pot, these will have the same flavor profile as the fried versions, but they're easier, neater, healthier, and equally tasty.

RICE AND NOODLES IN YOUR INSTANT POT

Rice and noodles make for excellent accompaniments to many of the recipes in this book. They are simple and quick to make in the Instant Pot. The types of rice and grains I generally use are short-grain rice, barley, black rice, and sweet rice. Regular white rice takes 13 minutes to cook, plus the time it takes for the Instant Pot to pressurize. Japgokbap, or Multigrain Rice and Beans (page 23), for example, will take slightly longer but is still faster than when cooked the stovetop.

Most (rice or wheat) noodles are added after the Instant Pot has finished pressure cooking because they only take a couple of minutes to cook. A good example is the Gamja Sujebi, or Umami Hand-Torn Noodles (page 64). Once the soup starts to boil, you'll be adding the hand-torn noodles to cook for just 5 minutes. Noodles do vary in cooking time, however, depending on what they are made from.

Essential Ingredients

Most Korean recipes depend on some common essential ingredients. Some are shelf-stable pantry ingredients like soy sauce, rice vinegar, and rice; some require refrigeration like scallions and kimchi. It's a good idea to stock your pantry and refrigerator with these items before starting to use the recipes in this book.

Instant Korean Pantry

Many of the staple ingredients, such as kimchi, short-grain rice, and gochujang, can be found in well-stocked grocery stores (check the International aisle). The rest can be found in many international, Asian, and Korean markets. With a few exceptions, they're inexpensive and have a long shelf life.

Mirin: This rice wine has a subtle sweetness that's perfect to add to the braising liquid for meat. It will last for 3 months in the pantry and 2 months longer in the refrigerator, but the taste begins to degrade after 3 months.

Soy Sauce: Due to its high salt content, soy sauce can last for a very long time if stored properly. But it will lose its quality over time, so it's best to use within the first year. There are endless varieties of soy sauce, but these are the most commonly used:

- **Joseon Soy Sauce or Soup Soy Sauce:** This traditional Korean soy sauce is much lighter in color and saltier than regular soy sauce. It's often used in soups to keep the broth light and clear and for making vegetable side dishes. It's made entirely from soy and brine with no wheat. You can make most Korean dishes using just this soy sauce, but be careful to use less than the regular soy sauce. This soy sauce will last longer (2 to 3 years) when refrigerated, but you can keep it in a dark pantry for up to 6 months. After that, it will lose quality and flavor.

- **Low-Sodium Soy Sauce:** Much lighter in taste, this soy sauce has 40 percent of its salt removed after brewing. You can use this soy sauce when making dishes if you want lower sodium content. This will last 3 months in the pantry and 2 years refrigerated.

- **Gluten-Free Soy Sauce:** This type of soy sauce is made from rice instead of wheat. Tamari is a commonly available gluten-free soy sauce. This will last for 3 months in the pantry and 2 years refrigerated.

Sesame Seeds: Great for topping and garnish, they will last for several months in the pantry and more than a year refrigerated. Like all nuts and seeds, they can become rancid if left at warm temperatures for too long. Sesame seeds are available raw or roasted (or you can roast them yourself).

Fish Sauce: Because fish sauce is fermented with a high salt content, it will last for up to 3 years in the refrigerator. Store-bought fish sauce can contain additives that may negatively affect the taste over time.

Gochujang: This very popular fermented sauce contains a lot of salt and will last more than 2 years inside the refrigerator. Homemade gochujang sauce can last for many years, but store-bought gochujang contains preservatives and additives that shorten the life span.

Rice Vinegar: With a lower level of acidity, rice vinegar is milder than many other types of vinegar. Vinegar will not expire and will last indefinitely in the refrigerator.

Rice Syrup: Used as a natural sweetener, it also gives a nice glazed finish to many dishes. Made from rice and barley malt powder, this syrup has a rich, grainy, and earthy flavor with a thick texture. It will last in the pantry for about a year.

Plum Syrup: Also called "maesil chung" in Korean, this fermented syrup is made from green apricot, plums, and sugar. Although I do not recommend substituting plum syrup for sugar when marinating or braising, it's a great condiment to include as a sweet flavor booster for side dishes. Stored at room temperature, this should last for more than a year.

Seaweed Paper: "Gim" in Korean is "seaweed paper," often served as a side dish to wrap rice or eaten as a snack. Basically, the seaweed has been chopped and dried into thin sheets. Several soup dishes, like the Tteokguk, or Rice Cake Soup (page 46), will require you to add crumbled gim for garnish. Gim will last in the freezer for up to 6 months if stored in an airtight sealed bag.

Dried Anchovy: There are two types of dried anchovy. The smaller one is used to make a side dish, whereas the bigger one is used to make soups and stocks. You can store the small anchovies in the refrigerator or freezer for up to 2 years. The bigger anchovies can be kept in an airtight bag or container in the pantry for about a year.

Dried Kelp: Also known as "kombu" or "dashida" in Japanese, kelp is an important ingredient for making soup bases and is widely used in many Korean dishes. Dried kelp will last for years if you keep it in a dry area.

Short-Grain Rice: Koreans only eat short-grain rice that's very sticky and starchy; a meal is never complete without rice. It's best to store rice in a cool, dry area and consume it within 3 to 6 months for the ultimate freshness.

Sweet Potato Noodles: Sold dried, these pantry-stable noodles are made from sweet potato starch. Also called glass noodles, these noodles are gluten-free and last for 3 years in the pantry.

(ALMOST) INSTANT BANCHAN

Banchan is a selection of small plates of vegetables and proteins served alongside a bowl of rice (with every single meal to balance out the flavors of the dishes), soup, and the main dish. Some banchan will be spicy, whereas others are milder. You will find several banchan recipes in this book, such as the Gyeran Jjim, or Steamed Eggs (page 18), easy to make on the weekend to enjoy throughout the week. Another banchan recipe that is great to make in advance is Gamja Jorim, or Braised Potatoes (page 24).

The main banchan served with every meal is kimchi. There are 200 varieties of kimchi, which range from nonspicy to very spicy. But banchan can and should vary, depending on seasonal ingredients and what else is on the menu. Most banchan is made in bulk, so it can be eaten throughout the week.

Fresh Ingredients

Korean dishes require a lot of fresh ingredients for flavor and for garnishes. It's important to remember that a Korean kitchen is a living one. There are many living organisms in foods like kimchi, gochujang, and doenjang, which have high levels of probiotics and live bacteria. Here is an overview of the core fresh ingredients used in many recipes.

Cabbage: There are two types of cabbage that are staples in Korean cooking. The first is napa cabbage, which is brined, seasoned, and fermented to make kimchi. Green cabbage is the second and is served either as a salad or steamed and paired with a side of doenjang.

Garlic: Garlic is a staple ingredient in Korean food and the most important aromatic used in recipes. Whole garlic cloves are used for soups, stews, and stocks. Minced garlic is used to season almost all savory dishes. It can be used in pickling, roasting, grilling, and sautéing. Garlic provides nutritional health benefits, aiding the digestive system.

Ginger: Although it is used less frequently than garlic, ginger is another common aromatic used in sauces, marinades, and kimchi. Due to its natural healing properties, ginger is made into tea to combat morning sickness, motion sickness, and many other stomach ailments. (Just a note: Making tea in the Instant Pot is wonderful because it allows more flavor and nutrient extraction from the ingredients in less time than the stovetop.)

Herbs: The fresh herbs most commonly used in Korea include kkae-ip (perilla leaves), ssuk-gat (crown daisy), and buchu (chives). These herbs are eaten raw, prepared as a side dish, added to kimchi, and used to flavor soups. They can also be made into savory pancakes.

Mushrooms: There are several varieties of mushrooms used in Korean cooking.

- Enoki mushrooms (paengi-buseot)
- King oyster mushrooms (songi-beoseot)
- Oyster mushrooms (neutari-beoseot)
- Rock ear mushrooms (seogi-beoseot)
- Shiitake mushrooms (pyogo-buseot)
- White mushrooms
- Wood ear mushrooms

Alliums: Scallions are the most common type of allium in Korean cuisine, used both as an aromatic and as a garnish in almost every Korean dish. White or yellow onions play an important role both in cooking and as a garnish. They are used fresh, sautéed, fermented, stewed, and in marinade recipes.

Tofu: Different types of tofu include silken, soft, medium, medium firm, firm and extra firm. For stews, you will be using the soft varieties. For braising, firm or extra firm work best because they hold their shape better.

Beef: The most commonly used cuts of beef in Korean cooking are thinly sliced deungsim (beef sirloin), ansim (beef tenderloin), kkot deungsim (rib eye roll), and chimasal yangji (flank steak), which is used to make Bulgogi. Galbi (short ribs) are cut two ways. The first is with the bone exposed on one short end with the meat filleted into a uniform layer. The other one is what's known as "flanken" in US butcher shops; it's cut crossways through the bones, resulting in long pieces of meat with (usually) three slices of bone running along one of the long sides.

Chicken: All parts of the chicken, including its organs, are used in Korean cooking. Fried chicken is very popular in Korea, especially paired with beer. It's also common to find the famous Samgaetang, or Ginseng Chicken Porridge (page 112), that's eaten as a medicinal and health food to help refresh the body. Braised chicken is usually made with spicy gochujang sauce and served family-style along with rice and soup.

Pork: Samgyeopsal, or "three-layer meat," is Korean-style pork belly that is grilled, braised, and boiled. Pork shoulder and pork ribs are used to make stews and for slow-braising dishes.

Seafood: Korea is surrounded by the ocean, so it is one of the main sources of food. Koreans love fresh seafood served raw, made into stews, or steamed. The recipes in this book call for mackerel and cod. I strongly recommend purchasing seafood at a Korean grocery store to find the widest selection.

ADAPTING RECIPES TO HIGH ALTITUDES

If you remember your science lessons, you know that the higher the altitude, the lower the atmospheric pressure. For the cook, the higher the altitude, the lower the boiling point of water, so foods will cook more slowly. Although the sealed interior of the Instant Pot helps make up for the lower atmospheric pressure, you'll still want to adjust cooking times if you live in the mountains. The Ultra and MAX models can be set to adjust automatically for high altitudes, but if you have a different model, you'll need to increase cooking times by 5 percent for every 1,000 feet above 2,000 feet. For very short cooking times, there will be virtually no difference, but for longer times, some adjustment is necessary. For instance, a dish that cooks for 30 minutes at sea level would cook for 31 minutes at 3,000 feet and 33 minutes at 4,000 feet.

About the Recipes

The recipes in this book were all tested using a 6-quart Instant Pot. They can be made in any model pot 6 quarts or larger (some can be made in the 3-quart mini; cooking times remain the same). Generally, they yield 4 to 6 servings. The first two recipe chapters are divided by type of dish: Appetizers and Sides (including banchan), and Soups and Stews. The others are grouped by main ingredient: Vegetables, Beef and Pork, and Poultry and Seafood.

Each recipe breaks down the total time necessary to make the recipe into prep time, sauté time (if any), and the time the pot takes to come to pressure, to pressure cook, and to release pressure.

To make it easier to find dishes that match your dietary needs, the recipes are flagged with the following labels: Vegan, Vegetarian, Gluten Free, and Soy Free. Always check ingredient packaging for gluten-free labeling (in order to ensure foods, especially oats, were processed in a completely gluten-free facility). In addition, so you can find recipes that fit within your time constraints, there are two labels: Make Ahead (for dishes that can be made the day before or easily frozen and reheated) and Super Fast (dishes that can be prepped and ready to serve in 30 minutes or less). Many of the recipes are followed by tips, which may include suggestions on prepping ingredients, shortcuts, advice on how to ensure a recipe's success, information on unusual ingredients, and simple variations that can be made by swapping ingredients. I hope these recipes inspire you to begin exploring the delights of Korean cooking, made faster and easier with the Instant Pot.

Appetizers and Sides

Gyeran Jjim | (Steamed Eggs) 18

Joomukbap | (Seasoned Rice Balls) 19

Yeongeun Jorim | (Braised Lotus Root) 20

Jangajji | (Korean Pickled Onion and Jalapeños) 22

Japgokbap | (Multigrain Rice and Beans) 23

Gamja Jorim | (Braised Potatoes) 24

Potato Salad 26

Sweet and Spicy Gochujang Cauliflower 28

Gaji Nameul | (Steamed Eggplant) 30

Homemade Mandu | (Korean Dumplings) 32

◄ HOMEMADE MANDU (KOREAN DUMPLINGS), page 32

Gyeran Jjim
(Steamed Eggs)

SERVES: 4 | Gluten Free, Soy Free, Super Fast

Gyeran Jjim, a soufflé-like (yet dairy-free) steamed egg dish, is typically served at Korean restaurants as a complimentary dish for Korean barbecue. It's a very popular side dish for children because of its soft, custard-like consistency. The taste is slightly savory and salty, and it pairs perfectly with rice. Add a few sesame seeds and some sesame oil at the very end for an extra nutty flavor.

PREP TIME:
5 minutes

PRESSURE BUILD:
5 minutes

PRESSURE COOK:
4 minutes

PRESSURE RELEASE:
6 minutes Natural, Quick Release remainder

TOTAL TIME:
25 minutes

1½ cups Korean stock (see Ingredient Tip, page 95) or water

5 large eggs, beaten

1 tablespoon saeujeot (salted fermented shrimp) or fish sauce, or 2 teaspoons coarse sea salt

1 scallion, both white and green parts, chopped

1. Pour 1 cup of water into the Instant Pot. Place a trivet inside.

2. In a 4-quart, oven-safe bowl or earthen pot that fits in the Instant Pot, mix together the stock and eggs.

3. Add the saeujeot, and mix well.

4. Sprinkle the scallion on top. Place a piece of aluminum foil over the bowl, and carefully place the bowl on the trivet in the Instant Pot. Lock the lid, and close the steam valve. Set the timer for 4 minutes on High Pressure.

5. When the timer sounds, natural release the steam for 6 minutes, then quick release the remainder. Open the lid. Serve immediately.

INGREDIENT TIP: Using kelp broth instead of water will create a deeper umami flavor, whereas saeujeot (salted fermented shrimp) adds a unique savory taste. You can use salt or fish sauce instead, but I highly recommend seeking out saeujeot.

Joomukbap
(Seasoned Rice Balls)

SERVES: 6 to 8 | Super Fast

This simple yet delectable recipe can be used just to make short-grain rice, which can also be formed into rice balls. Sometimes, the balls are filled with things like kimchi and Spam, spicy Bulgogi, sweet Bulgogi, or tuna with mayonnaise. These rice balls are perfect to pack for lunch or to take on a picnic. Using the Instant Pot for this recipe really saves time—12 minutes instead of almost an hour in the rice cooker.

PREP TIME:
10 minutes

PRESSURE BUILD:
5 minutes

PRESSURE COOK:
2 minutes

PRESSURE RELEASE:
10 minutes Natural, Quick Release remainder

TOTAL TIME:
30 minutes

2 cups short-grain rice

½ teaspoon coarse sea salt

1 tablespoon sesame oil

2 tablespoons rice seasoning mix (furikake)

Kimchi or pickled vegetables, for serving (optional)

1. Rinse the rice under cold water, and drain. Repeat this process until the water turns clear. Drain the rice at the final rinse, and put it directly in the Instant Pot.

2. Add 1¾ cups of water, lock the lid, and close the steam valve. Set the timer for 2 minutes on High Pressure.

3. When the timer sounds, natural release the steam for 10 minutes, then quick release the remainder. (It is very important that you quick release immediately after 10 minutes.) Open the lid.

4. Add the salt, oil, and rice seasoning mix. Mix well. Let the rice cool for about 3 minutes, or until cool enough to touch.

5. Using a spoon, scoop out about 2 tablespoons of the rice onto the palms of your hands. Roll it into a ball. Serve the rice balls with kimchi (if using).

VARIATION TIP: Try adding ¼ cup chopped carrots and ½ cup chopped onions mixed into the rice before cooking it. Then add the remaining ingredients, and shape it into the size of a golf ball or smaller. The size of the rice ball is your preference.

Yeongeun Jorim
(Braised Lotus Root)

SERVES: 6 | Vegan

Yeongeun Jorim is a sweet, crunchy, and savory side dish frequently eaten in autumn. The lotus root is first boiled to take out some of the starchy and bitter taste. What you are left with is a mildly sweet flavor and fibrous and crunchy texture that is super delicious. This makes for a great side dish to eat with rice; Miyeok Guk, or Seaweed Soup (page 52); and even Galbijjim, or Braised Short Ribs (page 90). Traditionally, the lotus root is simmered on the stovetop for almost an hour to achieve the soft, tender, yet still crunchy texture. Fortunately, this dish can be made in half the time with the Instant Pot.

PREP TIME:
5 minutes

SAUTÉ TIME:
5 minutes

PRESSURE BUILD:
10 minutes

PRESSURE COOK:
3 minutes and 1 minute

PRESSURE RELEASE:
5 minutes Natural, Quick Release remainder and 5 minutes Natural, Quick Release remainder

TOTAL TIME:
40 minutes

1 pound lotus root
1 tablespoon rice vinegar
5 tablespoons soy sauce
4 teaspoons rice wine
2 teaspoons granulated white sugar

2 teaspoons sesame oil, divided
3 tablespoons corn syrup or 2 tablespoons honey
1 tablespoon sesame seeds (optional)

1. Using a potato peeler, peel the skin off the lotus root, and cut off the tough ends. Cut it into ¼-inch-thick rounds. Put them directly into the Instant Pot.

2. Add the vinegar and enough water to cover the lotus. Lock the lid, and close the steam valve. Set the timer for 3 minutes on High Pressure.

3. When the timer sounds, natural release the steam for 5 minutes, then quick release the remainder. Open the lid.

4. Drain the lotus root, and rinse in cold water.

5. Return the lotus root to the Instant Pot, and add 1 cup of water, the soy sauce, rice wine, sugar, and 1 teaspoon of oil. Lock the lid, and close the steam valve. Set the timer for 1 minute on High Pressure.

6. When the timer sounds, natural release the steam for 5 minutes, then quick release the remainder.

7. Open the lid. Press the Sauté button, and set to High.

8. Once the screen reads HOT, add the remaining 1 teaspoon of oil and the corn syrup. Stir well, and allow the mixture to come to a boil, being mindful not to burn the sauce, about 5 minutes. Turn off the Instant Pot.

9. Sprinkle with sesame seeds for garnish before serving (if using).

INGREDIENT TIP: Lotus root (Yeongeun) is an excellent source of fiber and vitamin C, improves digestion, and helps regulate cholesterol. You can find lotus root at any Korean or Asian grocery store.

Jangajji

(Korean Pickled Onion and Jalapeños)

SERVES: 6 | Vegan

Jangajji, a type of spicy pickle, is often served at restaurants that are known for Korean barbecue or Seollungtang. It has a sweet yet salty flavor and crunchy texture that goes well with oxtail and any beef broth soups. Making it in the Instant Pot deepens the flavor of the sauce. This is one side dish that I always have in my refrigerator because it's super easy to make and lasts for more than 3 months if kept tightly sealed in a Mason jar. If you want to speed up the process, pour the pickling liquid into the vegetables when it's still very hot. Then you should be able to eat it the next day, but this will also cause the pickles to expire within a month.

PREP TIME:
25 minutes, plus 3 hours to cool and 3 to 4 days to pickle

PRESSURE BUILD:
5 minutes

PRESSURE COOK:
0 minutes

PRESSURE RELEASE:
2 minutes Natural, Quick Release remainder

TOTAL TIME:
35 minutes (plus 3 hours to cool and 3 to 4 days to pickle)

1 yellow onion, cut into bite-size pieces

4 jalapeños, cut into ½-inch pieces

1 cup soy sauce

½ cup granulated white sugar

½ cup rice vinegar

1. Let the onion and jalapeños dry on a paper towel for about 15 minutes, then put them in a 32-ounce Mason jar.

2. To make the pickling liquid, pour the soy sauce and sugar into the Instant Pot. Mix well. Lock the lid, and close the steam valve. Set the timer for 0 minutes on High Pressure.

3. When the timer sounds, natural release the steam for 2 minutes, then quick release the remainder. Open the lid.

4. Add the vinegar, and stir well. Turn off the Instant Pot. Let cool for 3 hours, or until cooled completely.

5. Pour the pickling liquid into the jar. Make sure that the vegetables are completely soaked in the pickling liquid. Cover the jar with a lid, and place it in a dark, cool area. Let sit at room temperature overnight before placing it inside the refrigerator to chill for 3 days for optimal eating.

Japgokbap
(Multigrain Rice and Beans)

SERVES: 4 | Vegan, Soy Free

"Japgok" means "multigrain" in Korean, and "bap" is "rice." This dish is a mixture of rice, grains, and beans that is heartier and more nutritious than plain rice. Some people add more than 10 different types of beans and grains, but here I start with a basic recipe. You can experiment with other rice, grains, and beans if you like. Just keep in mind that the ratio for the water to grains is 1:1.

PREP TIME:
5 minutes, plus overnight and 2 hours to soak

PRESSURE BUILD:
5 minutes

PRESSURE COOK:
20 minutes

PRESSURE RELEASE:
Quick Release

TOTAL TIME:
30 minutes (plus overnight and 2 hours to soak)

½ cup dried black beans
1 cup short-grain white rice
½ cup black sweet rice

¼ cup millet
¼ cup barley

1. Put the beans in a bowl, and cover with room-temperature water. Soak overnight. Drain.

2. In the Instant Pot, combine the beans, white rice, black rice, millet, and barley. Using cold running water, soak, wash, and drain all the ingredients until the water turns clear. You will need to repeat the rinsing process at least 5 times. At the final rinse, drain the grains completely.

3. Add 2½ cups of water, and let the grains soak in water for 2 hours. Then lock the lid, and close the steam valve. Set the timer for 20 minutes on High Pressure.

4. When the timer sounds, immediately quick release the steam. Open the lid. Mix the grains well before serving.

PREP TIPS: Soaking the black beans overnight helps them cook faster and more evenly with the rice and other grains. Once the rice has been cooked, it's very important that you quick release immediately. Otherwise, the rice will become mushy. To reheat this rice in the microwave, add 1 tablespoon water to the rice, and cover the bowl. Microwave on high for 1 to 1½ minutes, or until hot.

Gamja Jorim
(Braised Potatoes)

SERVES: 4 | Vegan, Make Ahead

"Gamja" means "potato" and "jorim" means "braised" in Korean. This is a side dish that can be enjoyed throughout the week for lunch or dinner. For best results, you will want to start by sautéing the potatoes so that the skin can crisp up before it gets braised with soy sauce and the other condiments. The taste is amazing, with the perfect balance of sweet and savory, and a nice creamy texture.

PREP TIME:
10 minutes

SAUTÉ TIME:
5 minutes and
5 minutes

PRESSURE BUILD:
5 minutes

PRESSURE COOK:
15 minutes

PRESSURE RELEASE:
10 minutes Natural Release, Quick Release remainder

TOTAL TIME:
55 minutes

1 pound baby potatoes
2 tablespoons vegetable oil
½ cup soy sauce
2 tablespoons light
   brown sugar
1 yellow onion
2 green chile peppers or
   ½ green bell pepper, seeded
   and chopped (optional)

2 garlic cloves, minced
1 tablespoon rice syrup
2 tablespoons sesame oil
1 teaspoon black pepper
2 scallions, both white and
   green parts, chopped
1 tablespoon sesame seeds

1. Wash the potatoes in cold water. Press the Sauté button, and set to High.

2. Once the screen reads HOT, pour the vegetable oil into the Instant Pot. Add the potatoes, and sauté for 5 minutes, or until the potatoes are slightly seared on all sides. Turn off the Sauté mode.

3. Add 1 cup of water, the soy sauce, and sugar. Lock the lid, and close the steam valve. Set the timer for 15 minutes on High Pressure.

4. When the timer sounds, natural release the steam for 10 minutes, then quick release the remainder. Open the lid.

5. Add the onion, chile peppers (if using), garlic, rice syrup, sesame oil, and pepper.

6. Press the Sauté button, and set to High. Let the mixture come to a boil. Cook for about 5 minutes, or until the sauce is reduced and the onions are soft.

7. Turn off the Instant Pot. Add the scallions and sesame seeds before serving.

PREP TIP: You can use any potatoes; just cut them into 2-inch dice after peeling. If using russet potatoes, cut into 2-inch dice, and be sure to soak them in water for at least 10 minutes and rinse before using to remove the starch.

Potato Salad

SERVES: 6 | Vegetarian, Gluten Free, Soy Free

Potato salad is an excellent side for grilled meats like Galbi and Bulgogi, so it is popular in Korean barbecue restaurants. Korean potato salad is creamy, yet has a nice crunch and sweetness coming from the apple, carrot, and cucumber. Try making a potato salad sandwich by layering finely chopped cabbage along with the potato salad in between two pieces of light fluffy Hokkaido (milk) bread. This is also known as an Inkigayo sandwich, named after the K-pop show that popularized it.

PREP TIME:
20 minutes, plus 1 hour to chill

PRESSURE BUILD:
10 minutes

PRESSURE COOK:
4 minutes and 6 minutes

PRESSURE RELEASE:
3 minutes Natural Release, Quick Release remainder and 4 minutes Natural Release

TOTAL TIME:
50 minutes (plus 1 hour to chill)

1 pound baby potatoes
3 large eggs
1 cucumber, thinly sliced
3 teaspoons coarse
  sea salt, divided
1 apple, cored and cut
  into 1-inch dice
1 carrot, cut into 1-inch
  pieces
½ cup mayonnaise
1 teaspoon granulated
  white sugar

1. In the Instant Pot, combine 1 cup of water and the potatoes.

2. Place a trivet on top, and put the eggs in the trivet. Fill a medium bowl with ice water to make an ice bath. Lock the lid, and close the steam valve. Set the timer for 4 minutes on High Pressure.

3. When the timer sounds, natural release the steam for 3 minutes, then quick release the remainder. Open the lid.

4. Remove the trivet and eggs, and place the eggs in the ice bath for 10 minutes.

5. Leave the potatoes in the Instant Pot. Lock the lid, and close the steam valve. Set the timer for 6 minutes on High Pressure.

6. When the timer sounds, natural release the steam for 4 minutes. Open the lid. Transfer the potatoes to a bowl. Let cool for 10 minutes.

7. Meanwhile, in a small bowl, combine the cucumber and 1 teaspoon of salt. Let sit for 10 minutes to release the water.

8. After 10 minutes, gently squeeze the cucumber, and drain.

9. Peel the cooled eggs, chop them, and add them to the cooled potatoes along with the apple, carrot, and drained cucumber.

10. Mix in the mayonnaise, sugar, and remaining 2 teaspoons of salt. (You can add more mayonnaise for a creamier consistency.) Combine well, and refrigerate for 1 hour before serving.

INGREDIENT TIPS: Try using a starchy potato like russet for a creamy texture. Using Persian, English, Japanese, or Korean cucumber would work best. But if you do use American cucumbers, make sure to remove the seeds and core, and peel the skin. Use either Fuji or Honeycrisp apples for the best flavor. Try adding raisins for extra sweetness.

Sweet and Spicy Gochujang Cauliflower

SERVES: 4 | Vegetarian, Make Ahead, Super Fast

You'll love this super healthy and quick side dish, which also works great for a busy weekday dinner when served with rice and kimchi. The Instant Pot helps the delicious sauce soak fully into the cauliflower, so that every bite will have a savory yet sweet taste that even the pickiest members of the family will love. The gochujang gives this recipe so much depth and flavor (which explains why it is such a stalwart in Korean cooking); halving the amount will make the recipe more kid friendly (less hot). This cauliflower dish can be eaten cold or hot and tastes great as leftovers.

PREP TIME:
5 minutes

SAUTÉ TIME:
2 minutes

PRESSURE BUILD:
5 minutes

PRESSURE COOK:
2 minutes

PRESSURE RELEASE:
Quick Release

TOTAL TIME:
20 minutes

3 tablespoons soy sauce

2 tablespoons honey

2 tablespoons granulated white sugar

1 tablespoon gochujang (fermented red pepper paste)

1 tablespoon rice syrup

1 teaspoon sesame oil

1 garlic clove, minced

1 teaspoon toasted sesame seeds

2 tablespoons vegetable oil

3 cups cauliflower florets (from 1 medium head)

1 scallion, both white and green parts, chopped

1. To make the sauce, in a small bowl, combine the soy sauce, honey, sugar, 2 tablespoons of water, the gochujang, rice syrup, sesame oil, garlic, and sesame seeds.

2. Press the Sauté button, and set to High.

3. Once the screen reads HOT, pour the vegetable oil into the Instant Pot. Add the cauliflower, and sauté, stirring occasionally, for 2 minutes. Turn off the Sauté mode.

4. Pour the sauce over the cauliflower, and mix well until coated. Lock the lid, and close the steam valve. Set the timer for 2 minutes on High Pressure.

5. When the timer sounds, immediately quick release the steam. Open the lid. Serve the cauliflower with the scallion sprinkled on top.

VARIATION TIP: The sweet and spicy sauce can also be used as a marinade for beef and chicken. Follow the same directions, but increase the cooking time for the proteins. If you would like to use tofu, make sure it's firm tofu, and skip the sauté process. Add the tofu and the sauce together to the Instant Pot, and cook for 2 minutes followed by a natural pressure release.

Gaji Nameul
(Steamed Eggplant)

SERVES: 4 | Vegan, Super Fast

The eggplants in this recipe (see Ingredient Tip) can stand up to the assertive flavors of garlic, ginger, and soy sauce. The eggplant here is steamed whole, and later cut into quarters. This classic summer side dish, made so much faster in the Instant Pot, can be served both warm and cold. It also makes for great leftovers but will need to be consumed within 3 days.

PREP TIME:
15 minutes

PRESSURE BUILD:
5 minutes

PRESSURE COOK:
1 minute

PRESSURE RELEASE:
Quick Release

TOTAL TIME:
25 minutes

2 medium Korean or Japanese eggplants (about 8 ounces total)
1 garlic clove, minced
1 scallion, both white and green parts, chopped
2 tablespoons soy sauce
1 teaspoon sesame oil
1 teaspoon gochugaru (Korean red chili flakes)
1 teaspoon sesame seeds
½ teaspoon minced fresh ginger
½ teaspoon granulated white sugar
¼ teaspoon black pepper

1. Cut the stems off the eggplants, but otherwise leave them whole.

2. Pour 1 cup of water into the Instant Pot, and drop in a steamer basket.

3. Put the eggplants in the steamer basket, lock the lid, and close the steam valve. Set the timer for 1 minute on High Pressure.

4. When the timer sounds, quick release the steam. Open the lid. Immediately take out the eggplants, place them on a plate, and let them cool to the touch, 5 minutes.

5. Once cool enough, quarter the eggplants lengthwise, then cut crosswise and into 4 equal parts. Transfer to a bowl.

6. To make the sauce, in a separate small bowl, combine the garlic, scallion, soy sauce, oil, gochugaru, sesame seeds, ginger, sugar, and pepper. Mix well.

7. Pour the sauce over the eggplant. Gently distribute the sauce throughout the eggplant, and serve immediately.

INGREDIENT TIP: For this recipe, purchase Korean or Japanese eggplants, which are slender and have a rich purple color. They are quick cooking because of their thin skin and are much sweeter tasting than the eggplant you may be accustomed to. Eggplants should be slightly firm to the touch. Find them easily in any Asian grocery store.

Homemade Mandu

(Korean Dumplings)

SERVES: 6 | Make Ahead, Super Fast

Dumplings, often served first thing on New Year's Day, are said to bring prosperity and luck. So, here's to getting some good luck in less than 30 minutes. All the ingredients are combined in a large bowl to make the filling and then the filling is individually wrapped in gyoza paper. The chives are a brilliant flavor addition; they perfectly complement the pork. And here's a bonus: You can steam all the dumplings and then freeze the leftovers. Just reheat them by either panfrying or adding them to soups like Soondubu, or Soft Tofu Stew (page 44).

PREP TIME:
15 minutes

PRESSURE BUILD:
5 minutes

PRESSURE COOK:
3 minutes

PRESSURE RELEASE:
Quick Release

TOTAL TIME:
25 minutes

FOR THE DUMPLINGS

- 1½ pounds ground pork (or see Variation Tip)
- 2 cups chopped chives
- 1 cup chopped Korean leeks (see Ingredient Tip) or scallions
- 2 large eggs, beaten
- 3 tablespoons soy sauce
- 2 tablespoons mirin
- 2 tablespoons coarse sea salt
- 2 tablespoons sesame oil
- 2 tablespoons minced garlic
- 2 teaspoons grated fresh ginger
- 1 teaspoon black pepper
- 1 (12-ounce) package 5-inch diameter pot sticker wrappers (or wonton wrappers)

1. **To Make the Dumplings:** In a large bowl, combine the pork, chives, leeks, eggs, soy sauce, mirin, salt, oil, garlic, ginger, and pepper. Using your hands, mix until everything is well incorporated.

2. Place a wrapper on a work surface, and place about 2 tablespoons of the filling in the middle of the wrapper. Wet the edges of the wrapper with either water or a beaten egg. Fold the wrapper in half, and pinch along the edges. (You can also bring the opposite ends of the dumpling to the center, and seal it there.) Repeat to make the remaining dumplings.

FOR THE DIPPING SAUCE

3 tablespoons
   soy sauce
1 tablespoon
   rice vinegar
1 teaspoon gochugaru
   (Korean red
   chili flakes)

3. To steam the dumplings, you can use either a stainless steel vegetable steamer or a bamboo steamer. Either cover in parchment paper, or spray with cooking spray. Pour 1 cup of water into the Instant Pot and place the steamer on top of the trivet.

4. Gently place the dumplings on top of the parchment paper in the steamer, so they don't touch each other. Cover the top of the steamer basket with a piece of cheesecloth or the bamboo lid. Lock the lid, and close the steam valve. Set the timer for 3 minutes on High Pressure.

5. When the timer sounds, quick release the steam. Open the lid. Carefully place the dumplings on a plate.

6. **To Make the Dipping Sauce:** In a small bowl, combine the soy sauce, vinegar, and gochugaru. Mix. Enjoy the dumplings with the dipping sauce.

VARIATION TIP: You can substitute the ground pork with 1½ pounds raw medium shrimp (chopped) or ground beef instead. Or you can make your dumplings vegetarian by using 14 ounces firm tofu and 8 ounces shiitake or enoki mushrooms.

INGREDIENT TIP: Korean leeks are bigger than scallions and have a mild onion-like flavor. Chinese chives (more garlicky and less delicate than chives) can also work in their place.

3

Soups and Stews

Seogogi Mu Guk | (Daikon Soup) 36

Kongbiji Jjigae | (Ground Soybean Stew) 38

Kimchi Samgyeopsal Jjim | (Braised Kimchi and Pork Belly) 40

Gamja Guk | (Egg Drop Potato Soup) 42

Soondubu | (Soft Tofu Stew) 44

Tteokguk | (Rice Cake Soup) 46

Kkori Gomtang | (Oxtail Soup) 48

Kimchi Jjigae | (Kimchi Stew) 50

Miyeok Guk | (Seaweed Soup) 52

Seolleongtang | (Milky Beef Bone Soup) 54

◀ KIMCHI SAMGYEOPSAL JJIM (BRAISED KIMCHI AND PORK BELLY), page 40

Seogogi Mu Guk
(Daikon Soup)

SERVES: 4 | Gluten Free

Seogogi Mu Guk is a light, clean, and refreshing soup that is served for breakfast, lunch, or dinner and is often offered for free along with rice in many Korean restaurants. It's frequently served as a counterpoint to all the rich grilled meats; in fact, the radish is supposed to help you digest. Cooking this soup in the Instant Pot brings out rich flavors from the meat and adds a soft texture to the radish or daikon. I like to pair it with grilled fish.

PREP TIME:
10 minutes

SAUTÉ TIME:
5 minutes

PRESSURE BUILD:
5 minutes

PRESSURE COOK:
8 minutes

PRESSURE RELEASE:
10 minutes Natural Release

TOTAL TIME:
40 minutes

1 teaspoon sesame oil

8 ounces beef brisket, beef round, or short rib, cut into bite-size pieces

½ Korean radish or daikon, peeled and cut into 2-inch dice (see Ingredient Tips)

1 tablespoon soup soy sauce (see Ingredient Tips)

2 teaspoons minced garlic

1 teaspoon fish sauce

1 teaspoon coarse sea salt, plus more as needed

2 scallions, both white and green parts, chopped

Short-grain rice, for serving

Kimchi, for serving (optional)

1. Press the Sauté button, and set to High.

2. Once the screen reads HOT, pour the oil into the Instant Pot. Add the beef and radish. Cook for about 5 minutes, or until the beef has browned and the radish has sweated out. Turn off the Sauté mode.

3. Add 6 cups of water, the soup soy sauce, garlic, fish sauce, and salt. Lock the lid, and close the steam valve. Set the timer for 8 minutes on High Pressure.

4. When the timer sounds, natural release the steam for 10 minutes. Open the lid.

5. Top with the scallions. Season with salt if needed. Ladle the soup into a bowl. Serve with rice, kimchi (if using), and side dishes.

PREP TIP: For a clean-tasting broth without any impurities and brown bits surfacing after the soup has been cooked, soak the brisket in cold water for 30 minutes prior to cooking. Discard the water, and cut the beef. Proceed with the directions in the recipe.

INGREDIENT TIPS: Ideally, in Korean cooking, when it's called for, soup soy sauce (guk ganjang) should be used. Soup soy sauce is lighter in color than regular soy sauce, much saltier, and naturally brewed. It can be ordered on Amazon if there isn't a Korean grocery store available. In a pinch, regular soy sauce can sub in for it. You'll just need to use half the amount and add salt to replace the other half. So, for example, if a recipe calls for 2 tablespoons soup soy sauce, you'll need 1 tablespoon regular soy sauce and 1 tablespoon salt. Soup soy sauce, like tamari, is generally gluten-free. Regular soy sauce is not.

Korean radish is much sweeter in taste when compared to daikon, but either can be used here.

Kongbiji Jjigae
(Ground Soybean Stew)

SERVES: 4 | Make Ahead

This is a comforting, creamy, nutty, warm stew that is often eaten during the cold winter months in Korea. This stew is made using soybeans that have been soaked overnight, pureed in a blender, and cooked. I like to add various nuts like walnuts, almonds, and cashews along with pine nuts. If you don't have any nuts, you can just use the soybeans, but I highly recommend that you add at least one of these nuts for a much more flavorful stew. Using the Instant Pot for this recipe deeply cooks and releases the aromatic flavors of the ingredients and significantly reduces the cooking time. Serve with rice.

PREP TIME:
15 minutes, plus 10 hours to soak

SAUTÉ TIME:
11 minutes

PRESSURE BUILD:
10 minutes

PRESSURE COOK:
1 minute and 3 minutes

PRESSURE RELEASE:
5 minutes Natural Release and 6 minutes Natural Release

TOTAL TIME:
50 minutes (plus 10 hours to soak)

½ cup dried soybeans

8 dried anchovies, guts and heads removed

1 (5-by-5-inch) piece dried kelp

¼ cup pine nuts (or any type of nut, up to a maximum of 1 cup)

⅓ cup chopped yellow onion

3 garlic cloves, minced

2 teaspoons sesame oil

6 ounces boneless pork shoulder, cut into bite-size pieces

1 cup kimchi (that has been ripened for at least 1 month), chopped

1 tablespoon soy sauce

½ teaspoon black pepper

2 tablespoons saeujeot (salted fermented shrimp) or fish sauce, or 2 teaspoons coarse sea salt

1 scallion, both white and green parts, chopped

1. Put the dried soybeans in a large bowl, and cover with 4 cups of water. Soak for at least 10 hours; the soybeans will expand and double in size.

2. When ready to cook, to make the anchovy broth, in the Instant Pot, combine the dried anchovies, kelp, and 4 cups of water. Lock the lid, and close the steam valve. Set the timer for 1 minute on High Pressure.

3. When the timer sounds, natural release the steam for 5 minutes. Open the lid. Reserving the liquid, strain the anchovies and kelp over a large bowl. Discard the solids.

4. Drain and rinse the soaked soybeans. You will need to repeat this process a couple of times so that the skins come off the beans. It's okay to eat the skins, and there is no need to discard all the skins.

5. Put the beans, 1 cup of water, and the pine nuts in a high-speed blender. Puree until smooth. You will have about 2 cups of creamy soybeans.

6. Press the Sauté button, and set to High.

7. Once the screen reads HOT, in the Instant Pot, combine the onion, garlic, and oil. Cook for 1 minute.

8. Add the pork, kimchi, soy sauce, and pepper. Cook, stirring occasionally, for about 10 minutes, or until the pork has browned and the kimchi has turned a little soft. Turn off the Sauté mode.

9. Add the soybean mix and saeujeot, then pour in the anchovy broth. If it's too thick, add ⅓ cup of water (it should be the consistency of porridge). Lock the lid, and close the steam valve. Set the timer for 3 minutes on High Pressure.

10. When the timer sounds, natural release the steam for 6 minutes. Open the lid.

11. Add the scallions, and lightly stir. Ladle the stew into a bowl. Serve immediately.

Kimchi Samgyeopsal Jjim
(Braised Kimchi and Pork Belly)

SERVES: 4 | Make Ahead

This savory and flavorful dish is a very popular comfort food in Korea, which will become even more popular in your house when you make it so quickly and easily in the Instant Pot. In fact, my family enjoys eating it a couple times a month, and it makes for great leftovers. All you will need is a bowl of rice to complete this meal and keep you satisfied. It pairs perfectly with Japgokbap, or Multigrain Rice and Beans (page 23).

PREP TIME:
10 minutes

SAUTÉ TIME:
5 minutes

PRESSURE BUILD:
5 minutes

PRESSURE COOK:
10 minutes

PRESSURE RELEASE:
10 minutes Natural Release

TOTAL TIME:
40 minutes

4 cups kimchi, cut into bite-size pieces

1 cup kimchi pickling liquid (optional)

1½ pounds pork belly, cut into bite-size pieces

3 tablespoons gochugaru (Korean red chili flakes)

2 tablespoons minced garlic

1½ tablespoons soy sauce

1 tablespoon grated fresh ginger

1 tablespoon doenjang (fermented soybean paste)

1 teaspoon granulated white sugar

1½ cups anchovy kombu broth (see Kongbiji Jjigae, page 38), vegetable broth, or rice water (obtained from rinsing rice)

2 scallions, both white and green parts, chopped

1. Press the Sauté button, and set to High.

2. Once the screen reads HOT, put the kimchi in the Instant Pot. Cook for 5 minutes.

3. Add the kimchi pickling liquid (if using). Turn off the Sauté mode.

4. Add the pork belly, gochugaru, garlic, soy sauce, ginger, doenjang, and sugar, followed by the broth. Lock the lid, and close the steam valve. Set the timer for 10 minutes on High Pressure.

5. When the timer sounds, natural release the steam for 10 minutes. Open the lid.

6. Stir in the scallions. Ladle the pork and kimchi into a large bowl. Serve family-style with rice.

INGREDIENT TIP: This recipe works best with very fermented kimchi, which is at least 1 month old. If you don't have any, though, you can use kimchi that has been sitting on the countertop overnight.

VARIATION TIP: Mackerel, black cod, or pike can be used instead of pork belly. You will need to adjust the pressure-cooking time to 5 minutes.

Gamja Guk
(Egg Drop Potato Soup)

SERVES: 4 | Gluten Free

Unlike Western-style potato soup, which is rich and creamy, the Korean version is made using clear broth, making it lighter and healthier. Traditionally, this soup is made with potatoes alone, but including the fish sauce, beef, and egg adds greater umami flavor and some protein while still keeping this dish light enough to enjoy regularly. The ingredients are simple, and the pressure-cooking process is quick enough for any rushed weeknight.

PREP TIME:
10 minutes

SAUTÉ TIME:
6 minutes

PRESSURE BUILD:
5 minutes

PRESSURE COOK:
6 minutes

PRESSURE RELEASE:
12 minutes Natural Release

TOTAL TIME:
40 minutes

1 tablespoon vegetable oil

4 ounces beef chuck, beef loin, flap steak, or beef stew meat, cut into small strips

1 tablespoon minced garlic

1 tablespoon soup soy sauce (see Daikon Soup, Ingredient Tip, page 37)

3 medium russet potatoes, peeled

½ yellow onion, chopped into 1-inch pieces

1 teaspoon fish sauce

2 large eggs, beaten

2 scallions, both white and green parts, chopped

Coarse sea salt

Black pepper

1. Press the Sauté button, and set to High.

2. Once the screen reads HOT, pour the oil into the Instant Pot. Add the beef, garlic, and soy sauce. Cook, turning the beef periodically, for about 5 minutes, or until the beef has browned on all sides.

3. Add the potatoes, and cook for 1 minute. Turn off the Sauté mode.

4. Add 5½ cups of water, the onion, and fish sauce. Lock the lid, and close the steam valve. Set the timer for 6 minutes on High Pressure.

5. When the timer sounds, natural release the steam for 12 minutes. Open the lid.

6. Pour the eggs into the soup, and add the scallions. Stir until the eggs are cooked through. Add salt and pepper to taste. Serve.

VARIATION TIP: To make this meatless (it still has fish sauce, so it is not vegetarian), use firm tofu or daikon, cut into 2-inch pieces.

Soondubu
(Soft Tofu Stew)

SERVES: 4 | Super Fast

Soondubu is a special type of tofu sold in Asian grocery stores. It comes in a tube-shaped package that will say "soondubu," but you can also use silken tofu. The word "soon" in soondubu means "pure" in Korean, which makes sense because this tofu is very soft and has not been strained or pressed. It makes for a hearty, spicy, warm, filling, and delicious comfort stew, which explains why it is one of the most popular dishes sold at any Korean restaurant. You can replace the ground pork or beef with a seafood mix (like shrimp, clams, and mussels), or make the dish vegetarian by using vegetable broth and assorted mushrooms.

PREP TIME:
10 minutes

SAUTÉ TIME:
8 minutes

PRESSURE BUILD:
5 minutes

PRESSURE COOK:
1 minute

PRESSURE RELEASE:
5 minutes Natural Release

TOTAL TIME:
30 minutes

1 cup kimchi, chopped into bite-size pieces, plus more for serving

¼ cup plus 2 tablespoons gochugaru (Korean red chili flakes)

2 tablespoons sesame oil

1 small yellow onion, chopped

2 tablespoons soy sauce

1 pound ground pork or beef

4 (12-ounce) tubes soondubu or silken tofu

8 ounces white mushrooms, sliced

4 (2-by-4-inch) pieces dried kombu (see Ingredient Tip)

2 tablespoons minced garlic

2 jalapeños, minced

4 large eggs (optional)

4 scallions, both white and green parts, chopped

Cooked rice, for serving

1. Press the Sauté button, and set to High.

2. Once the screen reads HOT, in the Instant Pot, combine the kimchi, gochugaru, oil, and onion. Sauté for 3 minutes, or until the onion has softened.

3. Add the soy sauce and pork. Cook for about 5 minutes, or until browned. Turn off the Sauté mode.

4. Pour in 4 cups of water, and add the soondubu, mushrooms, kombu, garlic, and jalapeños. Break the soondubu into large chunks. Lock the lid, and close the steam valve. Set the timer for 1 minute on High Pressure.

5. When the timer sounds, natural release the steam for 5 minutes. Open the lid.

6. Remove the kombu, and crack in the eggs (if using). The soup should be hot enough to cook the eggs in a few minutes. (If the broth isn't boiling hot, press the Sauté button again, and bring the soup to a boil before adding the eggs.)

7. Add the scallions, and lightly stir. Ladle the stew into individual bowls. Serve with rice and kimchi.

INGREDIENT TIP: Kombu is a sea vegetable or kelp that can be found in the dried seafood aisle of any Asian market. It is packed with nutrients and minerals, is great for making vegetarian soups, and provides an umami flavor to any dish.

Tteokguk

(Rice Cake Soup)

SERVES: 4 | Gluten Free

My grandma would always make this for New Year's Day. This is a symbolic dish that dates back hundreds of years and plays an important role in Korean culture. Traditionally, this soup is served on New Year's Day because it is believed to grant good luck for the year. In my grandmother's day, she would wake up extra early just to get started, and she would cook the beef alone for more than an hour so that the meat would soften. Now with the Instant Pot, you can carry on this tradition without sacrificing any sleep.

PREP TIME:
10 minutes,
plus
20 minutes
to soak

SAUTÉ TIME:
10 minutes

PRESSURE BUILD:
5 minutes

PRESSURE COOK:
15 minutes

PRESSURE RELEASE:
10 minutes
Natural
Release, Quick
Release
remainder

TOTAL TIME:
55 minutes
(plus
20 minutes
to soak)

FOR THE BEEF BROTH

8 ounces beef stew meat

5 garlic cloves, peeled

½ yellow onion

1. **To Make the Broth:** In the Instant Pot, combine the beef, 6 cups of water, the garlic, and onion. Lock the lid, and close the steam valve. Set the timer for 15 minutes on High Pressure.

2. When the timer sounds, natural release the steam for 10 minutes, then quick release the remainder. Open the lid.

3. Remove the beef, garlic, and onion. The broth should remain in the Instant Pot. Reserve the beef, let cool, and discard the onion and garlic.

4. Press the Sauté button, and set to High. Bring the broth to a boil.

5. **To Make the Broth Contents:** Cut the cooled beef into 1½-inch strips.

6. In a bowl, combine the beef, garlic, 2 scallions, the soup soy sauce, oil, sesame seeds, salt, and pepper. Mix well.

7. Once the broth is boiling, add the tteokguk tteok, and cook for about 5 minutes, or until soft.

FOR THE BROTH

CONTENTS

4 garlic cloves, minced

3 scallions, both white
and green parts,
chopped, divided

3 tablespoons
soup soy sauce
(see Daikon
Soup, Ingredient
Tip, page 37)

2 tablespoons
sesame oil

1 tablespoon
sesame seeds

1 tablespoon
coarse sea salt

1 teaspoon black
pepper

1 pound tteokguk
tteok (see Ingredient
Tip), soaked in water
for 20 minutes
and drained

2 large eggs, beaten

1 sheet roasted
Korean seaweed
(gim), crumbled

8. Add the eggs, and turn off the Instant Pot. Ladle the tteokguk tteok and broth into a bowl.

9. Top with the seasoned beef, seaweed, and remaining scallion.

INGREDIENT TIP: "Tteokguk tteok" translates to "rice cake soup rice cake." There are different types of rice cakes; some are flat and others are cylinders. For this recipe, you should use the flat oval rice cakes.

VARIATION TIP: Traditionally, this soup is garnished with a julienned panfried egg. You can make the egg garnish (jidan) by separating the whites and egg yolk and beating them in two different bowls. Heat up a skillet, and pour in a thin layer of vegetable or corn oil. Spread the yolk around the skillet, and cook it briefly. Repeat with the egg whites. Roll the cooked yolks and the cooked egg whites, and cut them into short thin strips to garnish the rice cakes.

Kkori Gomtang
(Oxtail Soup)

SERVES: 4 | Gluten Free, Soy Free

Did you know that oxtail comes from the tail of a cow rather than an ox? This soft, tender oxtail meat is mixed with broth and hot rice, perfect to pair with some ripened kimchi or Jangajji, or Korean Pickled Onion and Jalapeños (page 22). It's garnished with lots of scallions, and each person seasons their own soup with salt and pepper. The Korean radish gives the broth a refreshing taste. To successfully make this soup, it is important to soak the bones, blanch them, and clean the scum off in cold water. Cooking them for 25 minutes and doing a Natural Release achieves perfectly tender and juicy meat that is still intact on the bones.

PREP TIME:
10 minutes, plus 6 hours to soak and chill

PRESSURE BUILD:
10 minutes

PRESSURE COOK:
3 minutes and 25 minutes

PRESSURE RELEASE:
6 minutes Natural Release and 10 minutes Natural Release

3 pounds sliced oxtail (see Ingredient Tip)
1 pound Korean radish or daikon, halved lengthwise and into ½-inch-thick semicircles

6 garlic cloves, peeled
5 scallions, both white and green parts, chopped
Coarse sea salt
Black pepper
Cooked rice, for serving

1. In a large bowl, rinse the oxtail in cold running water; discard any bone fragments. Cover with water, and refrigerate for at least 6 hours. Change the water every 2 hours. Drain the oxtail, and transfer to the Instant Pot.

2. Add 4 cups of water. Lock the lid, and close the steam valve. Set the timer for 3 minutes on High Pressure.

3. When the timer sounds, natural release the steam for 6 minutes. Open the lid. Discard all the water, and rinse the oxtail under cold running water. Wash the pot clean so there is no scum or fat.

4. Return the oxtail to the Instant Pot, and add the radish, garlic, and 8 cups of water. Lock the lid, and close the steam valve. Set the timer for 25 minutes on High Pressure.

TOTAL
TIME: 1 hour
15 minutes
(plus
6 hours to
soak and chill)

5. When the timer sounds, natural release the steam for 10 minutes. Open the lid. Ladle the soup and oxtail into bowls.

6. Top with the scallions. Add salt and pepper to taste. Serve the dish with rice.

INGREDIENT TIP: Oxtails come precut and packaged in perfect sizes in Asian markets. A butcher can also cut it for you into 2- to 3-inch pieces. Oxtail has a deeply rich flavor when braised, so it is an excellent choice for making a beef stock.

PREP TIP: If you have some extra time, you can cool down the soup to room temperature, refrigerate it overnight, then remove the fat that has solidified on top.

Kimchi Jjigae

(Kimchi Stew)

SERVES: 4 | Make Ahead

Kimchi Jjigae is a staple stew in any Korean home that is usually served with fish, meat, and rice. The secret to making great-tasting Kimchi Jjigae is to first sauté the ripened kimchi with fatty pork or beef before adding the water. There's a trick with the water, too; using the water from rinsing the rice adds depth of flavor. After rinsing the rice two times, use the water from the third round of rinsing, and add it to the stew. Using the Instant Pot enhances and deepens the flavor because the soup gets absorbed into the kimchi and fully cooks without losing any taste.

PREP TIME:
5 minutes

SAUTÉ TIME:
20 minutes

PRESSURE BUILD:
5 minutes

PRESSURE COOK:
10 minutes

PRESSURE RELEASE:
15 minutes Natural Release

TOTAL TIME:
55 minutes

1 tablespoon canola, vegetable, or corn oil

2½ cups kimchi, chopped into bite-size pieces

8 ounces pork ribs or 1 (12-ounce) can luncheon meat like Spam, cut into 1-inch-thick slices

3 tablespoons gochugaru (Korean red chili flakes)

4 teaspoons minced garlic

½ cup kimchi pickling liquid (optional)

2 teaspoons fish sauce

2 teaspoons soy sauce

1 teaspoon granulated white sugar

1 (14-ounce) package medium firm tofu, cut into ½-inch-thick slices

3 scallions, both white and green parts, chopped

Cooked rice, for serving

1. Press the Sauté button, and set to High.

2. Once the screen reads HOT, in the Instant Pot, combine the oil and kimchi. Sauté for 3 minutes.

3. Add the pork, 4 cups of water, the gochugaru, garlic, kimchi pickling liquid (if using), fish sauce, soy sauce, and sugar. Cook for 10 minutes. Turn off the Sauté mode. Lock the lid, and close the steam valve. Set the timer for 10 minutes on High Pressure.

4. When the timer sounds, natural release the steam for 15 minutes.

5. Open the lid. Press the Sauté button, and set to High. Bring the stew to a boil, about 5 minutes.

6. Add the tofu, and cook for 2 minutes.

7. Add the scallions, and turn off the Instant Pot. Serve the stew immediately with rice.

VARIATION TIP: If you would prefer to make this a pescatarian stew, replace the pork with canned tuna. You can also create umami flavors by adding anchovy broth instead of plain water as a great soup base.

Miyeok Guk
(Seaweed Soup)

SERVES: 4 or 5 | Gluten Free

Korean seaweed soup is one of the easiest soups to make. It's also known as the "birthday soup" because it's traditionally served to a woman who had just given birth. Made using brown seaweed, it provides many nutrients and health benefits for nursing mothers. Because of this association with childbirth, Koreans eat this soup first thing in the morning on their birthdays. But because it's so comforting and delicious, Koreans also enjoy it throughout the year. Making this soup in the Instant Pot creates deeper flavors in the soup and a softer texture to the seaweed.

PREP TIME:
5 minutes, plus
20 minutes to soak

SAUTÉ TIME:
7 minutes

PRESSURE BUILD:
5 minutes

PRESSURE COOK:
20 minutes

PRESSURE RELEASE:
10 minutes Natural Release

TOTAL TIME:
50 minutes (plus 20 minutes to soak)

1½ grams (0.05 ounces) dried wakame or dried sea mustard

1 tablespoon sesame oil, plus 1 teaspoon

8 ounces beef brisket, round, or skirt steak, cut into bite-size pieces

1 teaspoon minced garlic

2 tablespoons soup soy sauce (see Daikon Soup, Ingredient Tip, page 37)

½ teaspoon fish sauce

1. Put the dried seaweed in a large bowl, and cover in room-temperature water. Soak for 20 minutes. Then drain and rinse several times in cold running water. Drain once more, and squeeze the water out. Cut into bite-size pieces.

2. Press the Sauté button, and set to High.

3. Once the screen reads HOT, in the Instant Pot, combine 1 tablespoon of oil, the beef, and garlic. Cook for 5 minutes, or until the beef has browned.

4. Add the seaweed. Sauté for 2 minutes.

5. Add 6 cups of water, the soup soy sauce, and fish sauce. Turn off the Sauté mode. Lock the lid, and close the steam valve. Set the timer for 20 minutes on High Pressure.

6. When the timer sounds, natural release the steam for 10 minutes. Open the lid. Ladle the soup into a bowl.

7. Drizzle with the remaining 1 teaspoon of oil before serving.

VARIATION TIP: Try this recipe with mussels instead of beef. I like to buy prepackaged New Zealand greenshell mussels in the half shell because they are cleaned and ready to cook. Add 8 ounces mussels along with water after you have sautéed the seaweed.

Seolleongtang
(Milky Beef Bone Soup)

SERVES: 6 | Gluten Free, Soy Free

This soup has "milky" in the name, but that's due to the rich texture and color of the soup, not because it has any dairy in it. Seolleongtang is a staple Korean soup that is usually served during the cold winter months. It does take some advance planning, but the taste is worth it. And making it in the Instant Pot does save a significant amount of time while still extracting the sumptuous flavors. It has a rich flavor that is super nourishing and warms you up instantly. Traditionally served in a clay bowl, there are a couple of condiments that are typically added for extra flavor, like chopped scallions, sea salt, black pepper, spicy paste, radish kimchi, and ripened napa cabbage kimchi. Make it heartier by serving with rice or thin noodles.

PREP TIME:
5 minutes,
plus 6 hours
to soak

PRESSURE BUILD:
25 minutes

PRESSURE COOK:
5 minutes
(parboil),
5 hours, and
40 minutes

2 pounds beef marrow bones, a mixture of knuckles and foot bones (you can also use leg bones, tail bones, head bones, or a mix of the bones; see Ingredient Tip)

1 pound beef brisket or flank
3 bunches scallions, both white and green parts, chopped
Coarse sea salt
Black pepper

1. Wash the bones in cold running water. Put them in a large bowl, and cover with cold water. Soak for at least 6 hours, changing the water every 2 hours. Drain, and wash them again in running water. Transfer to the Instant Pot.

2. Add enough water to submerge the bones. Lock the lid, and close the steam valve. Set the timer for 5 minutes on High Pressure, and parboil the bones.

3. When the timer sounds, natural release the steam for 10 minutes. Open the lid.

4. Rinse the bones in cold running water. Discard the scum.

PRESSURE
RELEASE:
10 minutes
Natural
Release,
30 minutes
Natural
Release, and
3 minutes Natural Release

TOTAL TIME:
7 hours (plus
6 hours
to soak)

5. Return the clean bones to the Instant Pot. Fill with water to the MAX line. Lock the lid, and close the steam valve. Set the timer for 5 hours on High Pressure.

6. When the timer sounds, natural release the steam for 30 minutes. Open the lid.

7. Add the brisket, lock the lid, and close the steam valve. Set the timer for 40 minutes on High Pressure.

8. When the timer sounds, natural release the steam for 3 minutes. Open the lid.

9. Discard the bones. Take out the brisket, and slice thinly.

10. Using a spoon, skim the fat off the top of the broth, or put the cooled broth in the refrigerator overnight, then spoon off the solidified fat. Ladle the soup into a big bowl.

11. Add the sliced brisket (and some cooked rice or noodles if desired).

12. Garnish with the scallions. Add salt and pepper to taste.

INGREDIENT TIP: You can call your local butcher shop and ask them to reserve the beef marrow bones and knuckle or foot bones in advance. Asian markets will sell them in the freezer aisle in a bag. You can freeze any leftover bones for later use.

Vegetable Dishes

Hobak Jook | (Squash Porridge) 58

Dubu Jorim | (Spicy Braised Tofu) 59

Pat Jook | (Sweet Red Bean Porridge) 60

Beosot Bap | (Mushroom Rice) 62

Gamja Sujebi | (Umami Hand-Torn Noodles) 64

Yachae Japchae | (Vegetarian Sweet Potato Noodles) 66

Beosot Deulkkae Tang | (Mushroom Perilla Seed Casserole) 68

Cabbage with Tofu Roll Casserole 70

◂ GAMJA SUJEBI (UMAMI HAND-TORN NOODLES), page 64

Hobak Jook

(Squash Porridge)

SERVES: 4 | Vegan, Gluten Free, Soy Free, Make Ahead

Hobak Jook is served for breakfast in Korea or given to someone recovering from illness or surgery. It's also popular to serve to toddlers because of its natural sweetness. Feel free to add sunflower seeds and pine nuts for garnish.

PREP TIME:
20 minutes

SAUTÉ TIME:
10 minutes

PRESSURE BUILD:
5 minutes

PRESSURE COOK:
10 minutes

PRESSURE RELEASE:
5 minutes Natural Release, Quick Release remainder

TOTAL TIME:
50 minutes

1 (about 4-pound) kabocha or butternut squash, washed, halved, and seeded

1 teaspoon coarse sea salt

1 teaspoon granulated white sugar

¼ cup mochiko (sweet rice flour)

1. Pour 1 cup of water into the Instant Pot. Place a trivet inside, and carefully place the squash halves on top. Set the timer for 10 minutes on High Pressure.

2. When the timer sounds, natural release the steam for 5 minutes, then quick release the remainder. Open the lid.

3. Using oven mitts, remove the squash from the Instant Pot. Let cool for 10 minutes. Peel off the skin, and chop the squash into smaller chunks.

4. Return the squash to the pot, and add 3 cups of water, the salt, and sugar. Using an immersion blender, puree the squash. (If you do not have an immersion blender, put the squash water, sugar, and salt in a blender. Puree, then return to the Instant Pot).

5. Press the Sauté button, and set to High. Bring the squash puree to a boil, stirring often to avoid burning it.

6. Once the squash puree starts to boil, add the mochiko. Stir for 3 minutes; it is done when you achieve a creamy consistency similar to an oatmeal. Turn off the Instant Pot. This porridge can be served hot or cold and can be frozen for up to 1 month.

Dubu Jorim
(Spicy Braised Tofu)

SERVES: 4 | Vegan, Make Ahead, Super Fast

This spicy, vegan-friendly tofu dish is a satisfying meal you can quickly make after work with minimal prep work and cleanup. This tastes even better the next day as leftovers. It goes perfectly with rice and kimchi.

PREP TIME:
5 minutes

SAUTÉ TIME: 5 to 10 minutes

PRESSURE BUILD:
5 minutes

PRESSURE COOK:
0 minutes

PRESSURE RELEASE:
Quick Release

TOTAL TIME: 20 to 25 minutes

1 (14-ounce) package extra-firm tofu, cut into ½-inch-thick slices
¼ cup soy sauce
1 tablespoon sesame oil
2 teaspoons gochugaru (Korean red chili flakes)
1 teaspoon mirin or cooking wine

1 teaspoon sesame seeds
1 teaspoon minced garlic
1 teaspoon plum extract or granulated white sugar
2 tablespoons vegetable oil
2 scallions, both white and green parts, finely chopped

1. Pat the tofu dry.

2. To make the sauce, in a medium bowl, combine the soy sauce, ¼ cup of water, the sesame oil, gochugaru, mirin, sesame seeds, garlic, and plum extract.

3. Press the Sauté button, and set to High.

4. Once the screen reads HOT, pour the vegetable oil into the Instant Pot. Working in batches, add the tofu. Cook for about 2 minutes per side, or until lightly browned. Transfer to a plate. Once all the tofu slices have been browned, return them to the Instant Pot. Turn off the Sauté mode.

5. Pour the sauce all over the tofu. Lock the lid, and close the steam valve. Set the timer for 0 minutes on High Pressure.

6. When the timer sounds, quick release the steam. Open the lid. Serve the tofu on a plate.

7. Garnish with the scallions.

Pat Jook

(Sweet Red Bean Porridge)

SERVES: 4 | Vegan, Gluten Free, Soy Free

Pat Jook reminds me of snowy days in Korea when it's often served for breakfast or a midday snack because it is super warm and comforting. Historically, people often ate Pak Jook because it kept them full despite the shortage of rice. To eat this as a dessert, just add more sugar to sweeten the porridge. Garnish with pine nuts, chestnuts, and rice cake balls (see Variation Tip).

PREP TIME:
5 minutes, plus overnight to soak

SAUTÉ TIME:
5 minutes

PRESSURE BUILD:
5 minutes

PRESSURE COOK:
5 minutes and 10 minutes

PRESSURE RELEASE:
5 minutes Natural Release, Quick Release remainder and 15 minutes Natural Release

TOTAL TIME:
55 minutes (plus overnight to soak)

1 cup adzuki beans, soaked in water overnight
2 tablespoons sweet rice flour (see Hobak Jook, Ingredient Tip, page 58)

¼ cup granulated white sugar
1 teaspoon coarse sea salt

1. Drain and rinse the soaked beans. Put them in the Instant Pot.

2. Add 4 cups of water. Lock the lid, and close the steam valve. Set the timer for 5 minutes on High Pressure.

3. When the timer sounds, natural release the steam for 5 minutes, then quick release the remainder. Open the lid. Drain the beans.

4. Return the beans to the pot, and add 4 cups of water, the flour, sugar, and salt. Mix well. Lock the lid, and close the steam valve. Set the timer for 10 minutes on High Pressure.

5. When the timer sounds, natural release the steam for 15 minutes. Open the lid.

6. Using an immersion blender, puree the bean mixture until smooth. (If using a traditional blender rather than an immersion blender, you may have to do this in 2 batches and will then return the porridge to the Instant Pot).

7. Press the Sauté button, and set to High. Bring the porridge to a boil for 5 minutes. Turn off the Instant Pot. Ladle the porridge into a bowl, along with any garnish you choose.

VARIATION TIP: To make rice cake balls, gather ⅓ cup sweet rice flour, 2 teaspoons granulated white sugar, ⅛ teaspoon coarse sea salt, and 3½ tablespoons hot water. In a bowl, combine the sweet rice flour, sugar, and salt. Mix. Slowly add the hot water, and when the mixture is cool enough, use your hands to make a dough. Roll it into ¾-inch pieces. Pour 3 cups of water into the Instant Pot. Add the rolled rice cake balls. Set the timer for 0 minutes on High Pressure, and do a quick release. Rinse and drain the rice balls.

Beosot Bap

(Mushroom Rice)

SERVES: 4 or 5 | Vegan

This healthy, vegan recipe came about because of the abundance of mushrooms that once proliferated all over Korea. Feel free to use any combination and variety of mushrooms for this recipe. Using the Instant Pot to make this recipe is ideal because the mushroom flavors don't evaporate and, rather, cook right into the rice. The mushrooms and rice come out moist and perfectly cooked.

PREP TIME:
10 minutes, plus 1 hour to soak

PRESSURE BUILD:
5 minutes

PRESSURE COOK:
5 minutes

PRESSURE RELEASE:
8 minutes Natural Release, Quick Release remainder

TOTAL TIME:
30 minutes (plus 1 hour to soak)

FOR THE MUSHROOM RICE

2 cups short-grain white rice

1 cup sweet white rice

4 ounces dried shiitake mushrooms

7 ounces enoki mushrooms

7 ounces oyster mushrooms, cut into 1-inch pieces

4 king oyster mushrooms, cut into 1-inch pieces

1. **To Make the Mushroom Rice:** Using the inner pot of the Instant Pot, wash the rice, then fill with water to completely cover the top of the rice. Let soak for 1 hour. Drain, and return the rice to the pot. At the same time, put the shiitake mushrooms in a bowl, and cover with 2½ cups of room-temperature water. Soak for 30 minutes. Do not discard this water.

2. To the rice, add the 2½ cups of the shiitake mushroom water.

3. Place the shiitake mushrooms, enoki mushrooms, oyster mushrooms, and king oyster mushrooms on top of the rice. Lock the lid, and close the steam valve. Set the timer for 5 minutes on High Pressure.

4. When the timer sounds, natural release the steam for 8 minutes, then quick release the remainder. Open the lid.

FOR THE SAUCE

½ cup chopped scallions

1 garlic clove, minced

½ jalapeño, chopped

2 tablespoons soy sauce

1 tablespoon sesame oil

1 teaspoon sesame seeds

5. **To Make the Sauce:** In a bowl, mix together the scallions, garlic, jalapeño, soy sauce, 1 tablespoon of water, the oil, and sesame seeds.

6. Mix together the rice and mushrooms. Serve in a bowl with a side of sauce.

Gamja Sujebi

(Umami Hand-Torn Noodles)

SERVES: 4

Sujebi is a popular Korean-style pasta noodle soup that is made by breaking the flour dough pieces by hand and not a machine. Historically, rice was expensive in Korea, so many people ate Sujebi because it was less costly but equally filling. The umami flavor comes from the dried kelp and anchovies. Cooking this in the Instant Pot is so much quicker and results in a more deeply flavored dish.

PREP TIME:
15 minutes

SAUTÉ TIME:
5 minutes

PRESSURE BUILD:
10 minutes

PRESSURE COOK:
1 minute and 1 minute

PRESSURE RELEASE:
5 minutes Natural Release and Quick Release

TOTAL TIME:
40 minutes

FOR THE NOODLES

3 cups all-purpose flour

2 tablespoons vegetable oil

1 teaspoon coarse sea salt

14 dried anchovies, head and guts removed

6 (5-by-5-inch) dried kelp pieces

3 medium russet potatoes, peeled and cut into bite-size pieces

5 garlic cloves, minced

1 small yellow onion, sliced

3 tablespoons soup soy sauce (see Daikon Soup, Ingredient Tip, page 37)

2 tablespoons fish sauce

Coarse sea salt

2 scallions, both white and green parts, chopped

1 tablespoon sesame oil

1. **To Make the Noodles:** In a large bowl, mix together the flour, 1 cup of water, the vegetable oil, and salt for 10 minutes, or until the dough is no longer sticky and forms into a smooth ball. Cover the bowl with plastic wrap, and keep refrigerated while completing the next steps.

2. In the Instant Pot, combine the dried anchovies, dried kelp, and 4 cups of water. Lock the lid, and close the steam valve. Set the timer for 1 minute on High Pressure.

3. When the timer sounds, natural release the steam for 5 minutes. Open the lid.

FOR THE SAUCE

6 tablespoons
  soy sauce

1 scallion, both
  white and green
  parts, chopped

2 garlic cloves, minced

2 teaspoons
  sesame oil

1½ teaspoons
  chopped chile
  pepper or jalapeño

¼ teaspoon
  black pepper

4. Discard the anchovies and kelp. Add the potatoes, garlic, and onion. Lock the lid, and close the steam valve. Set the timer for 1 minute on High Pressure.

5. When the timer sounds, quick release the steam. Open the lid.

6. Press the Sauté button, and set to High.

7. Once the screen reads HOT, add the soy sauce and fish sauce. Add salt to taste.

8. When the mixture comes to a boil, add the noodles: hold the dough in one hand, and use the other one to tear off 2-inch-by-½-inch pieces. Flatten them into a pasta-like thickness before adding them to the broth. Boil for 5 minutes, or until the noodles are opaque and tender. Turn off the Instant Pot.

9. **To Make the Sauce:** In a mixing bowl, stir together the soy sauce, scallion, garlic, sesame oil, chile pepper, and black pepper. Ladle the noodles into a bowl.

10. Add the scallions and sesame oil. Serve the noodles with a side of sauce.

VARIATION TIP: Add 1 teaspoon gochugaru to the sauce to give this dish a spicy kick.

Yachae Japchae
(Vegetarian Sweet Potato Noodles)

SERVES: 4 | Vegetarian, Gluten Free, Super Fast

Japchae is a popular traditional noodle dish in Korea, often served at weddings and celebrations. Historically, Japchae was eaten during royal banquets and parties because it was considered a luxurious and elegant dish. But now, you can make Japchae in the Instant Pot, which will impress your guests in no time flat. If you'd like a protein boost and aren't a vegetarian, consider adding marinated Bulgogi on the bottom of the pot before adding the noodles and vegetables; just mix thoroughly at the end.

PREP TIME:
15 minutes

PRESSURE BUILD:
5 minutes

PRESSURE COOK:
2 minutes

PRESSURE RELEASE:
Quick Release

TOTAL TIME:
25 minutes

FOR THE NOODLES

8 ounces sweet potato noodles (see Ingredient Tip)
2 tablespoons vegetable oil
1 carrot, julienned
½ medium red, yellow, or green bell pepper, cored and chopped

½ yellow onion, thinly sliced
1 cup shiitake mushrooms, stemmed and thinly sliced
½ cup chopped scallions, both white and green parts, or Asian chives
½ cup baby spinach

1. **To Make the Noodles:** Using scissors, cut the noodles into 8-inch lengths. Put them in a large bowl, and cover with water. Make sure all the noodles are immersed in water. Soak for about 3 minutes. Drain.

2. **To Make the Sauce:** While the noodles are soaking, in a medium bowl, mix together ½ cup of water, the tamari, sugar, sesame oil, sesame seeds, mirin, garlic, ginger, salt, and pepper.

3. Pour the vegetable oil into the Instant Pot. Add the noodles first, then on top, place the carrot, bell pepper, onion, mushrooms, scallions, and spinach.

FOR THE SAUCE

5 tablespoons tamari (or soy sauce, if gluten is not an issue)

1 tablespoon granulated white sugar

1 tablespoon sesame oil

1 tablespoon sesame seeds, plus more for garnish

1 tablespoon mirin

1 teaspoon minced garlic

1 teaspoon grated ginger

½ teaspoon coarse sea salt

¼ teaspoon black pepper

4. Pour half of the sauce over the vegetables. Lock the lid, and close the steam valve. Set the timer for 2 minutes on High Pressure.

5. When the timer sounds, quick release the steam. Open the lid.

6. Add the remaining sauce, and mix carefully.

7. Plate the noodles and vegetables, garnished with extra sesame seeds. Serve immediately.

INGREDIENT TIP: The sweet potato noodles are sold dried in a long package at Asian grocery stores. They are inexpensive, tasty, and healthy, with a nice chewy texture.

Beosot Deulkkae Tang

(Mushroom Perilla Seed Casserole)

SERVES: 4 | Gluten Free, Super Fast

Lots of vegan dishes are made using mushrooms because they are grown so abundantly in Korea and because of their many health benefits for memory, skin, heart, energy level, and bones. Plus this soup tastes like the way a warm blanket feels, with a nutty, savory, and creamy unique flavor and texture that is healthy and comforting to eat. It's delicious served with kimchi. If you can't find perilla seed powder, use finely ground sesame seeds.

PREP TIME:
10 minutes

SAUTÉ TIME:
10 minutes

PRESSURE BUILD:
5 minutes

PRESSURE COOK:
1 minute

PRESSURE RELEASE:
Quick Release

TOTAL TIME:
30 minutes

1 tablespoon vegetable oil
1 pound fresh assorted mushrooms (oyster, enoki, cremini, white button, shiitake, beech)
1 medium yellow onion, thinly sliced
2 garlic cloves, minced
4 cups vegetable stock
1½ tablespoons fish sauce

1 teaspoon coarse sea salt
1½ cups sweet rice flour (see Hobak Jook, Ingredient Tip, page 58)
¾ cup perilla seed powder (see Ingredient Tip)
¼ cup plus 2 tablespoons chives, cut into 2-inch pieces

1. Press the Sauté button, and set to High.

2. Once the screen reads HOT, in the Instant Pot, combine the oil, mushrooms, onion, and garlic. Cook for 2 minutes. Turn off the Sauté mode.

3. Add the vegetable stock, fish sauce, and salt. Lock the lid, and close the steam valve. Set the timer for 1 minute on High Pressure.

4. When the timer sounds, quick release the steam. Open the lid.

5. Press the Sauté button, and set to High. Bring the soup to a boil.

6. Meanwhile, in a bowl, mix together the flour, perilla seed powder, and ⅓ cup of water until smooth.

7. Add the mixture to the Instant Pot, and stir for 2 minutes.

8. Add the chives. Turn off the Instant Pot. Stir thoroughly. Serve the soup with a side of kimchi.

INGREDIENT TIP: Perilla seeds come from an herb that is known for its medicinal and health benefits. Ground, roasted perilla seeds are used in Korean cooking as an ingredient and as a garnish. If kept in a dry, cool place in a sealed container, they will keep fresh for a year.

Cabbage with Tofu Roll Casserole

SERVES: 5 | Vegetarian, Gluten Free, Super Fast

This all-in-one meal contains healthy vegetables and brown rice all wrapped up in a neat cabbage roll package. The Instant Pot perfectly prepares the cabbage so that it's not wilted but steamed and crunchy. Feel free to add a dollop of gochujang into the sauce for a spicy kick to this dish. For a nonvegetarian option, you can add cooked, marinated, finely chopped Bulgogi or ground beef to the filling.

PREP TIME:
15 minutes

PRESSURE BUILD:
10 minutes

PRESSURE COOK:
0 minutes and 1 minute

PRESSURE RELEASE:
Quick Release and Quick Release

TOTAL TIME:
30 minutes

FOR THE CABBAGE
12 green cabbage leaves

FOR THE SAUCE
1 cup tomato paste
4½ tablespoons tamari
3½ tablespoons plum syrup or granulated white sugar

3 tablespoons rice syrup (ssal-jocheong, sold in Asian markets) or light honey
5 garlic cloves, minced
1 teaspoon ground ginger

1. **To Make the Cabbage:** Pour 1 cup of water into the Instant Pot, and place the steamer basket inside.

2. Place the cabbage leaves inside the basket. Lock the lid, and close the steam valve. Set the timer for 0 minutes on High Pressure.

3. When the timer sounds, quick release the steam. Open the lid.

4. Carefully take out the cabbage leaves and steamer basket. Discard the water inside the pot.

5. **To Make the Sauce:** In a small bowl, mix together 1½ cups of water, the tomato paste, tamari, plum syrup, rice syrup, garlic, and ginger.

FOR THE FILLING

½ cup finely
chopped leeks

½ yellow onion,
finely chopped

½ carrot, finely
chopped

½ cup white
mushrooms, chopped

1 (14-ounce) package
extra-firm tofu,
drained and
water squeezed,
finely chopped

1 cup cooked
brown rice

1 scallion, both white
and green parts,
finely chopped

6. **To Make the Filling:** In a large bowl, combine the leeks, onion, carrot, mushrooms, tofu, and rice.

7. Add 3 tablespoons of the sauce to the filling, and mix well.

8. Place a scoop (about ⅓ cup) of the filling on the center of a cabbage leaf. Fold in the sides, and roll up. Repeat for all of the cabbage leaves.

9. Place the rolls inside the Instant Pot, seam-side down, and spoon the remaining sauce all over the cabbage rolls. Lock the lid, and close the steam valve. Set the timer for 1 minute on High Pressure.

10. When the timer sounds, quick release the steam. Open the lid. Serve the rolls on a large plate.

11. Garnish with the scallion.

INGREDIENT TIP: Rice syrup (ssal-jocheong) is used in Korean cuisine as a natural sweetener and to add a shiny glaze to dishes.

5

Beef and Pork Dishes

Yachae Gogi Jook | (Beef and Vegetable Porridge) 74

Jeyuk Bokkeum | (Spicy Pork Bulgogi) 76

Bossam | (Boiled Pork Belly) 78

Maeun Dwaeji Galbi | (Sticky Pork Ribs) 80

Dwaeji Gogi Gan Jang Jorim | (Soy-Braised Pork Belly) 82

Galbi Tang | (Beef Short Rib Medley) 84

Jangjorim | (Soy-Braised Beef with Eggs) 86

Ground Beef Bulgogi with Rice 88

Galbijjim | (Braised Short Ribs) 90

Yookgaejang | (Spicy Shredded Beef and Vegetable Chowder) 92

Bulgogi Jungol | (Bulgogi Casserole with Noodles) 94

Gamja Tang | (Spicy Pork Bone Jumble) 96

◂ MAEUN DWAEJI GALBI (STICKY PORK RIBS), page 80

Yachae Gogi Jook
(Beef and Vegetable Porridge)

SERVES: 4 | Make Ahead

My mom would often make Yachae Gogi Jook for breakfast and serve it with a side of Jangjorim, or Soy-Braised Beef with Eggs (page 86) and kimchi. It was super comforting to eat this in the morning and drizzle some of the Jangjorim sauce all over the porridge. Kids tend to love this jook because of its soft texture and mild taste. And it's so much quicker and easier to make in the Instant Pot; the stovetop method requires more than an hour and constant stirring.

PREP TIME:
10 minutes, plus 1 hour to soak in advance

SAUTÉ TIME:
13 minutes

PRESSURE BUILD:
5 minutes

PRESSURE COOK:
5 minutes

PRESSURE RELEASE:
10 minutes Natural Release, Quick Release remainder

TOTAL TIME:
45 minutes (plus 1 hour to soak)

1 cup short-grain rice
2 tablespoons sesame oil
8 ounces (90 percent lean) ground beef
1 tablespoon sesame seeds, plus more for garnish
1 teaspoon soy sauce
¼ cup chopped yellow onion
3 garlic cloves, minced
⅓ cup finely chopped carrots
⅓ cup finely chopped red, yellow, or orange bell pepper
¼ cup finely chopped zucchini
2 tablespoons coarse sea salt
1 scallion, both white and green parts, chopped

1. Put the rice in a medium bowl, and cover with water. Soak for 1 hour. Drain.

2. Press the Sauté button, and set to High.

3. Once the screen reads HOT, in the Instant Pot, combine the oil, beef, sesame seeds, and soy sauce. Cook for about 4 minutes, or until the beef has browned.

4. Add the onion and garlic. Cook for 3 minutes, or until the onion turns translucent.

5. Add the soaked rice. Stir, and cook for 4 minutes.

6. Add the carrots, bell pepper, zucchini, and salt. Stir, and cook for 2 minutes. Turn off the Sauté mode.

7. Add 6 cups of water. Lock the lid, and close the steam valve. Set the timer for 5 minutes on High Pressure.

8. When the timer sounds, natural release the steam for 10 minutes, then quick release the remainder. Open the lid. Ladle the porridge into a bowl.

9. Garnish with the scallions and sesame seeds.

10. Serve the porridge with kimchi and Jangjorim (page 86) if you'd like.

Jeyuk Bokkeum
(Spicy Pork Bulgogi)

SERVES: 6

Jeyuk Bokkeum, a.k.a. Dwegi Bulgogi, is a spicy marinated pork featuring lots of garlic and ginger. "Jeyuk" means "pork," and "bokkeum" means "stir-fry." It is an extremely popular dish in Korea, often eaten with red-leaf lettuce, ssam sauce, and rice. Making it in the Instant Pot builds better flavor and creates a juicier texture than the stovetop version. You can omit the jalapeño and add less gochujang and gochugaru for a less spicy version. Serve it with rice, garnished with scallions and sesame seeds.

PREP TIME:
10 minutes, plus 3 hours to marinate

SAUTÉ TIME:
5 minutes

PRESSURE BUILD:
5 minutes

PRESSURE COOK:
2 minutes

PRESSURE RELEASE:
1 minute Natural Release, Quick Release remainder

TOTAL TIME:
25 minutes (plus 3 hours to marinate)

- ½ cup gochujang (fermented red pepper paste)
- ¼ cup soy sauce
- 3 tablespoons rice wine or mirin
- 3 tablespoons granulated white sugar
- ½ apple or Asian pear, grated
- 2 tablespoons gochugaru (Korean red chili flakes)
- 2 tablespoons minced garlic
- 1 tablespoon honey
- 1 tablespoon sesame oil
- 1 tablespoon grated fresh ginger or 1 teaspoon ginger powder
- 2 teaspoons black pepper
- 3 pounds pork butt or shoulder, cut into ½-inch-thick pieces
- 1 medium yellow onion, thinly sliced
- 4 scallions, both white and green parts, cut into 4-inch pieces
- 1 small jalapeño, seeded and thinly sliced

1. In a large bowl, mix together the gochujang, soy sauce, rice wine, sugar, apple, gochugaru, garlic, honey, sesame oil, ginger, and pepper.

2. Add the pork, onion, scallions, and jalapeño. Cover with plastic wrap, and marinate for 3 hours in the refrigerator.

3. Put the pork and marinade in the Instant Pot. Lock the lid, and close the steam valve. Set the timer for 2 minutes on High Pressure.

4. When the timer sounds, natural release the steam for 1 minute, then quick release the remainder. Open the lid.

5. Press the Sauté button, and set to High. Cook for 5 minutes. Turn off the Instant Pot. Using tongs, take the pork out, and place it on rice.

6. Garnish with chopped scallions and sesame seeds if you choose.

INGREDIENT TIP: Try buying presliced pork Bulgogi, which is widely available in Asian grocery stores. If you cannot find it easily, slice the pork when it is half frozen. You will have a much easier time cutting the meat.

Bossam

(Boiled Pork Belly)

SERVES: 4

Bossam is a quick and easy dish that is usually eaten with spicy radish salad, salted napa cabbage, and salted fermented shrimp (see Variation Tip). To wrap it up, take a piece of napa cabbage in the palm of your hand, then place a piece of pork belly on top, along with a couple pieces of radish salad and about ¼ teaspoon salted fermented shrimp. This wrap is called "ssam" in Korean and is a popular, hearty, and nutritious way to eat either steamed or barbecue proteins. Made in the Instant Pot, Bossam comes out extra tender, juicy, and flavorful from all of the aromatics.

PREP TIME:
15 minutes

PRESSURE BUILD:
5 minutes

PRESSURE COOK:
15 minutes

PRESSURE RELEASE:
10 minutes Natural Release, Quick Release remainder

TOTAL TIME:
50 minutes

2 pounds skin-on pork belly
½ yellow onion
5 scallions, white parts only
6 garlic cloves, peeled
1 (2-inch) piece ginger, sliced
8 black peppercorns
2 tablespoons doenjang (fermented soybean paste)
2 teaspoons instant coffee
6 cups water
Salted napa cabbage, saeujeot (salted fermented shrimp), and musaengchae (spicy radish salad), for serving (optional) (see Variation Tip)

1. In the Instant Pot, combine the pork, onion, scallions, garlic, ginger, peppercorns, doenjang, instant coffee, and water. Lock the lid, and close the steam valve. Set the timer for 15 minutes on High Pressure.

2. When the timer sounds, natural release the steam for 10 minutes, then quick release the remainder. Open the lid. Transfer the pork belly to a cutting board. Let rest for about 10 minutes, or until cool enough to touch.

3. Cut the pork into 1-inch pieces. Serve with salted napa cabbage or lettuce, saeujeot, and musaengchae, if desired.

VARIATION TIP: Serve this with a side of salted shrimp sauce and spicy radish salad, and on napa cabbage. To make the salted shrimp sauce, mix 3 tablespoons salted fermented shrimp with 1 tablespoon vinegar, 1 chopped scallion, and ½ chopped jalapeño. For the spicy radish, cut 4 ounces radish into matchsticks about ¼-inch thick. In a bowl, mix the radish with 1 teaspoon coarse sea salt. Set aside for 20 minutes, or until the radish releases liquid. Discard the excess liquid, but do not rinse. Mix in 2 tablespoons gochugaru, 2 teaspoons garlic, 1 teaspoon sugar, 1 tablespoon fish sauce, 2 teaspoons sesame seeds, and 1 chopped scallion. Toss well, and serve. To brine the napa cabbage, sprinkle the washed leaves with ½ teaspoon salt on each leaf, and let sit for 20 minutes, or until the leaves have softened. Quickly rinse the leaves under water, shake off excess water, and serve.

Maeun Dwaeji Galbi
(Sticky Pork Ribs)

SERVES: 6

This pork rib is fall-off-the-bone tender, juicy, sweet, spicy, and so tasty that it will become your new favorite way to eat ribs. Using the Instant Pot helps the marinade seep deeply into the pork, creating an umami burst of irresistible flavor. You can adjust the level of spicy taste by adding less of the gochujang. This dish pairs perfectly with rice and kimchi, as well as with Potato Salad (page 26) and Sweet and Spicy Gochujang Cauliflower (page 28).

PREP TIME:
10 minutes, plus 6 hours to overnight to marinate

SAUTÉ TIME:
10 minutes

PRESSURE BUILD:
10 minutes

PRESSURE COOK:
15 minutes and 5 minutes

PRESSURE RELEASE:
10 minutes Natural Release and 10 minutes Natural Release

½ cup grated peeled Asian pear or red apple
¼ cup soy sauce
¼ cup water
¼ cup dark brown sugar
¼ cup gochujang (fermented red pepper paste)
2 tablespoons rice wine
1 tablespoon minced garlic
2 teaspoons ground ginger
½ teaspoon black pepper

3 pounds pork ribs, membrane removed, cut into riblets
4 russet potatoes, peeled and cut into large chunks
1 small daikon or Korean radish, peeled and cut into 3-inch dice (about 2 cups)
1 small yellow onion, cut into large chunks
1 small carrot, cut into large chunks

4. To make the marinade, in a large bowl, combine the pear, soy sauce, water, sugar, gochujang, rice wine, garlic, ginger, and pepper.

5. Add the ribs, and thoroughly cover them with the marinade. Cover the bowl with plastic wrap, and refrigerate for 6 hours to overnight.

6. Put the ribs and marinade in the Instant Pot. Lock the lid, and close the steam valve. Set the timer for 15 minutes on High Pressure.

TOTAL TIME: 1 hour 10 minutes (plus 6 hours to overnight to marinate)

7. When the timer sounds, natural release the steam for 10 minutes. Open the lid.

8. Add the potatoes, daikon, onion, and carrot. Lock the lid, and close the steam valve. Set the timer for 5 minutes on High Pressure.

9. When the timer sounds, natural release the steam for 10 minutes. Open the lid. Press the Sauté button, and set to High. Let the sauce boil and thicken slightly for 10 minutes. Turn off the Instant Pot. Gently stir. Serve the ribs on a plate with a side of rice and kimchi.

Dwaeji Gogi Gan Jang Jorim
(Soy-Braised Pork Belly)

SERVES: 6 | Make Ahead

This is a true potluck and party favorite in Korea. You can easily double the recipe to feed a crowd. The Instant Pot tenderizes the pork and makes this dish even more flavorful and tasty than when made with traditional cooking methods. Try adding some gochujang for some heat. Serve it over rice, drizzled with the delicious sauce, and a side of kimchi.

PREP TIME:
5 minutes

SAUTÉ TIME:
10 minutes

PRESSURE BUILD:
10 minutes

PRESSURE COOK:
1 minute and 10 minutes

PRESSURE RELEASE:
Quick Release and 5 minutes Natural Release, Quick Release remainder

TOTAL TIME:
45 minutes

3 pounds skin-on, lean pork belly (trim some of the fat) or pork shoulder, cut into 2-inch pieces

¼ cup plus 1 tablespoon granulated white sugar

¼ cup soy sauce

2 tablespoons minced garlic

2 tablespoons grated fresh ginger or 1 tablespoon ground ginger

1 tablespoon sesame oil

1 tablespoon mirin or rice wine

1 tablespoon sesame seeds

1. In the Instant Pot, combine the pork belly and 1 cup of water. Lock the lid, and close the steam valve. Set the timer for 1 minute on High Pressure.

2. When the timer sounds, quick release the steam. Open the lid. Drain the pork belly in a colander.

3. Return the pork belly to the Instant Pot. Press the Sauté button, and set to High. Cook for about 5 minutes, or until slightly seared. Turn off the Sauté mode.

4. To make the sauce, in a medium bowl, combine sugar, soy sauce, ¼ cup of water, the garlic, ginger, oil, mirin, and sesame seeds.

5. Pour the sauce over the pork belly. Lock the lid, and close the steam valve. Set the timer for 10 minutes on High Pressure.

6. When the timer sounds, natural release the steam for 5 minutes, then quick release the remainder.

7. Open the lid. Press the Sauté button, and set to High. Boil the sauce for 5 minutes, or until thickened. Turn off the Instant Pot.

8. Spoon the pork belly on top of rice, and drizzle with the sauce. Enjoy with a side of kimchi.

Galbi Tang

(Beef Short Rib Medley)

SERVES: 6 | Gluten Free, Soy Free, Make Ahead

Rich and savory, Galbi Tang fills you up and tastes incredible during the cold winter months. My grandmother would prepare this early in the morning and have it simmering on the stovetop all day until it was ready to eat for dinner. The whole house would have the aroma of Galbi Tang as the bones slowly released all the nutrients and delicious, hearty flavors began bonding with the daikon and garlic. Fortunately, the Instant Pot allows you to enjoy this soup in about 1 hour. Pressure cooking the beef releases the natural juices in less time and helps bring the whole soup together quite nicely.

PREP TIME:
5 minutes, plus 1 hour to soak

PRESSURE BUILD:
10 minutes

PRESSURE COOK:
5 minutes and 20 minutes

PRESSURE RELEASE:
Quick Release and 15 minutes Natural Release, Quick Release remainder

TOTAL TIME:
1 hour (plus 1 hour to soak)

4 pounds bone-in short ribs
1 medium daikon or
   Korean radish, cut
   into 4-inch pieces
1 medium yellow onion

5 garlic cloves, peeled
2 scallions, both white and
   green parts, chopped
Coarse sea salt
Black pepper

1. Rinse the short ribs in cold water to remove any debris and bone fragments. Put them in a bowl, and cover with water. Soak for 1 hour. Drain.

2. Put the short ribs in the Instant Pot, and add about 4 cups of water, or enough to completely cover the meat. Lock the lid, and close the steam valve. Set the timer for 5 minutes on High Pressure.

3. When the timer sounds, quick release the steam. Open the lid. Drain the short ribs in a colander. Rinse in cold water to clean off the scum and debris.

4. Return the short ribs to the Instant Pot, and add the daikon, onion, garlic, and 8 cups of water. Lock the lid, and close the steam valve. Set the timer for 20 minutes on High Pressure.

5. When the timer sounds, natural release the steam for 15 minutes, then quick release the remainder. Open the lid. Serve the soup topped with the scallions. Add salt and pepper to taste. This soup can be refrigerated overnight so that the fat solidifies on top, and you can remove it using a spoon. It will freeze nicely for 3 months and keep fresh in the refrigerator for up to 5 days.

PREP TIP: To achieve a cleaner wholesome soup, you have the option of soaking the short ribs in water for at least 4 hours. Rinse and parboil the ribs (steps 2 and 3) to release the scum and debris. After thoroughly cleaning the bones, they are now ready to cook.

Jangjorim
(Soy-Braised Beef with Eggs)

SERVES: 6 | Make Ahead

Jangjorim is a staple side dish in Korea that is often served with soup, rice, and other side dishes. I used to take Jangjorim to school along with rice, and it was such a hearty meal. The dish is slightly sweet but mostly salty and savory, brought to perfect balance by the hard-boiled eggs and peppers. If you want to make it extra spicy, add one sliced jalapeño, and enjoy a little kick with the meat.

PREP TIME:
15 minutes

SAUTÉ TIME:
20 minutes

PRESSURE BUILD:
5 minutes

PRESSURE COOK:
5 minutes and
15 minutes

PRESSURE RELEASE:
Quick Release and 5 minutes Natural Release, Quick Release remainder

TOTAL TIME: 1 hour

6 large eggs
1 pound beef brisket, cut into 3-inch pieces
8 garlic cloves, peeled
1 (3-inch) piece ginger, peeled and cut into 3 pieces

1 cup soy sauce
¼ cup granulated white sugar
10 shishito peppers, stemmed

1. Pour 1 cup of water into the Instant Pot. Place the trivet inside. Fill a bowl with ice water to make an ice bath.

2. Carefully place the eggs on top of the trivet. Lock the lid, and close the steam valve. Set the timer for 5 minutes on High Pressure.

3. When the timer sounds, quick release the steam. Open the lid.

4. Remove the trivet and eggs, place the eggs in the ice bath to cool for 5 minutes, then peel.

5. In the Instant Pot, combine the beef, 3½ cups of water, the garlic, and ginger. Lock the lid, and close the steam valve. Set the timer for 15 minutes on High Pressure.

6. When the timer sounds, natural release the steam for 5 minutes, then quick release the remainder. Open the lid.

7. Add the soy sauce, sugar, eggs, and shishito peppers. Press the Sauté button, and boil for 20 minutes, or until the meat breaks off easily. Turn off the Instant Pot. Serve warm with rice and side dishes. Refrigerate the leftovers. You can eat them cold the next day, or warm them up in the microwave.

VARIATION TIP: If you prefer, you can replace the eggs with quail eggs, and use jalapeños, halved, instead of shishito peppers.

Ground Beef Bulgogi with Rice

SERVES: 4 | Make Ahead

This all-in-one dinner makes for a perfect weeknight go-to. By using the pot-in-pot method, you can cook two dishes at once. While the rice is cooking to a nice fluffy texture, the beef is soaking in all that nice Bulgogi flavor. This dish is freezer friendly, so it is a great recipe to make in advance. You can also use ground turkey instead of beef.

PREP TIME:
10 minutes

SAUTÉ TIME:
5 minutes

PRESSURE BUILD:
5 minutes

PRESSURE COOK:
3 minutes

PRESSURE RELEASE:
10 minutes
Natural Release,
Quick Release remainder

TOTAL TIME:
35 minutes

1 tablespoon olive, canola, or vegetable oil
1 pound (90 percent lean) ground beef
¼ cup plus 1 tablespoon soy sauce
3 garlic cloves, minced
2 tablespoons granulated white sugar or honey
1 tablespoon sesame oil

2 teaspoons sesame seeds
1 teaspoon grated fresh ginger or ½ teaspoon ground ginger
1 teaspoon black pepper
1 scallion, both white and green parts, chopped
2½ cups short-grain rice
Kimchi and side dishes, for serving

1. Press the Sauté button, and set to High.

2. Once the screen reads HOT, pour the olive oil into the Instant Pot. Add the beef, and cook for about 5 minutes, or until the pink doesn't show. Turn off the Sauté mode. Discard extra liquid if necessary.

3. In a small bowl, combine ½ cup of water, the soy sauce, garlic, sugar, sesame oil, sesame seeds, ginger, pepper, and scallion.

4. Pour the mixture all over the beef, and stir well.

5. Wash the rice several times until the water becomes clear.

6. In a bowl that fits into the pot, combine the rice and 2 cups of water.

7. Place a trivet over the ground beef, and place the bowl of rice on top of the trivet. Lock the lid, and close the steam valve. Set the timer for 3 minutes on High Pressure.

8. When the timer sounds, natural release the steam for 10 minutes, then quick release the remainder. Open the lid.

9. Using oven gloves, carefully take out the rice and trivet.

10. Divide the rice into individual portions, and top with the beef. Serve with kimchi and Korean side dishes.

PREP TIP: I bought my stackable 6-inch insert pan from Amazon to do pot-in-pot cooking. You can also use a 6-inch stainless steel cake pan or bowl to fit the Instant Pot.

Galbijjim
(Braised Short Ribs)

SERVES: 5

Traditionally, this dish takes more than 4 hours to make on the stovetop. The short ribs are cooked over low heat and simmered for a long time to achieve their intense flavors. The Instant Pot reduces this time significantly, and what you'll end up with is a super flavorful sauce with a sweet soy-braised taste and tender, fall-off-the-bone meat. Including the chestnuts and jujubes adds wonderful flavor and texture to the dish. Serve with rice.

PREP TIME:
10 minutes, plus 1 hour to soak

SAUTÉ TIME:
10 minutes

PRESSURE BUILD:
15 minutes

PRESSURE COOK:
3 minutes and 15 minutes

PRESSURE RELEASE:
Quick Release and 10 minutes Natural Release, Quick Release remainder

3½ pounds bone-in short ribs
½ apple or Asian pear, peeled, cored, and chopped
¼ cup soy sauce
¼ cup packed dark brown sugar
3 tablespoons rice wine or mirin
2 tablespoons minced garlic
¼ yellow onion, chopped

1 tablespoon sesame oil
4 black peppercorns or 1 tablespoon black pepper
2 large carrots, chopped into bite-size pieces
8 chestnuts, peeled (optional)
8 dried jujubes (optional)
Sesame seeds, for serving (optional)

1. Put the short ribs in a large bowl, and cover with water. Soak for 1 hour to draw out the red liquid (which looks like blood) from the meat. Drain and rinse the ribs. Transfer to the Instant Pot.

2. Add 3 cups of water. Lock the lid, and close the steam valve. Set the timer for 3 minutes on High Pressure.

3. To make the sauce, put 2 cups of water, the apple, soy sauce, sugar, rice wine, garlic, onion, sesame oil, and peppercorns in a blender. Puree until smooth.

4. When the timer sounds, quick release the steam. Open the lid. Carefully take out the pot. You will notice scum floating on top of the water. Drain and rinse the ribs. Wash the pot thoroughly.

**TOTAL
TIME:** 1 hour
5 minutes
(plus 1 hour
to soak)

5. Return the ribs to the Instant Pot, and pour in the sauce. Stir gently. Lock the lid, and close the steam valve. Set the timer for 15 minutes on High Pressure.

6. When the timer sounds, natural release the steam for 10 minutes, then quick release the remainder.

7. Open the lid. Press the Sauté button, and set to High. Once the sauce starts to boil, add the carrots, chestnuts (if using), and jujubes (if using). Cook for about 10 minutes, or until the carrots are soft and tender. Turn off the Instant Pot.

8. Using a slotted spoon, place the ribs and vegetables in a big shallow bowl.

9. Garnish with sesame seeds (if using).

VARIATION TIP: If you don't have jujubes and chestnuts, add more carrots and onions. Or for an extra delectable twist, add potatoes and daikon to soak up the sauce.

Yookgaejang
(Spicy Shredded Beef and Vegetable Chowder)

SERVES: 6 | Make Ahead

Yookgaejang is a very popular smoky, spicy, healthy Korean medley enjoyed for lunch or dinner. It is served with rice and simple banchan because the dish itself is already very hearty. The beef is traditionally boiled for more than an hour on the stovetop but takes just 20 minutes in the Instant Pot. Yookgaejang tastes even better the next day when the vegetables and beef have had time to soak and release their juices. If you have leftovers, just portion them out into a zip-top bag, and freeze them. They'll last for 4 days in the refrigerator and 3 months in the freezer. Serve this with rice and simple sides.

PREP TIME:
15 minutes

SAUTÉ TIME:
20 minutes

PRESSURE BUILD:
10 minutes

PRESSURE COOK:
20 minutes

PRESSURE RELEASE:
10 minutes Natural Release, Quick Release remainder

TOTAL TIME: 1 hour 20 minutes

FOR THE BRISKET

1 pound beef brisket

4 garlic cloves, peeled

1 medium yellow onion, halved lengthwise

FOR THE SAUCE

⅓ cup gochugaru (Korean red chili flakes)

6 garlic cloves, minced

2½ tablespoons soup soy sauce (see Daikon Soup, Ingredient Tip, page 37)

1 tablespoon gochujang (fermented red pepper paste)

1 tablespoon coarse sea salt

2 teaspoons sesame seeds, crushed

1 teaspoon granulated white sugar

1½ teaspoons black pepper

1. **To Make the Brisket:** Put the brisket in a large bowl, and cover with water. Soak for 10 minutes. Drain.

2. In the Instant Pot, combine the brisket, 6 cups of water, the garlic, and onion. Lock the lid, and close the steam valve. Set the timer for 20 minutes on High Pressure.

FOR THE VEGETABLES

8 ounces mung bean sprouts, rinsed

2 daepa (large scallions), cut into 2-inch pieces, or 3 scallions, chopped into quarters

5 fresh or dried (and soaked) shiitake mushrooms, sliced

5 ounces gosari, soaked and cut into 2½-inch pieces (optional) (see Ingredient Tips)

3. When the timer sounds, natural release the steam for 10 minutes, then quick release the remainder. Open the lid.

4. Using a slotted spoon, take out the brisket, and discard the onion and garlic. Leave the broth in the Instant Pot.

5. Using your hands or a fork, shred the brisket.

6. **To Make the Sauce:** In a medium bowl, combine the gochugaru, garlic, soy sauce, gochujang, salt, sesame seeds, sugar, and pepper. Mix well.

7. **To Make the Vegetables:** In a mixing bowl, mix the sauce in with the bean sprouts, daepa, mushrooms, and gosari (if using) to combine well.

8. Press the Sauté button, and set to High. Bring the broth to a boil.

9. Add the vegetable sauce mixture, and stir well. Boil for 15 minutes.

10. Add the shredded brisket, and boil for another 5 minutes. Turn off the Instant Pot. Ladle the dish into a bowl.

INGREDIENT TIPS: Gosari is bracken, an edible green, and can be found dried in a package. You will need to rehydrate the gosari by soaking it in hot water until softened. Traditionally, it's best to use daepa (large scallion) rather than scallions for this dish. Daepa elevates the dish and brings out a deeper taste with its sweet onion flavor. But if it isn't available, you can use regular scallions.

Bulgogi Jungol
(Bulgogi Casserole with Noodles)

SERVES: 6 | Make Ahead

Bulgogi is widely known as a meat to barbecue, but you can also make it in the form of a casserole and serve it as a one-pot dish to your family. To make it casserole worthy, all you have to do is add vegetables and sweet potato noodles and pour beef broth over the Bulgogi. Bulgogi is sold at all Korean grocery stores presliced and frozen. To save time and effort, I always buy the presliced version instead of slicing it myself at home.

PREP TIME:
15 minutes, plus 2 hours to chill

PRESSURE BUILD:
5 minutes

PRESSURE COOK:
10 minutes

PRESSURE RELEASE:
5 minutes Natural Release, Quick Release remainder

TOTAL TIME:
40 minutes (plus 2 hours to chill)

⅓ cup grated peeled apple or Asian pear

¼ cup plus 1 tablespoon soy sauce

3 garlic cloves, minced

3 tablespoons granulated white sugar

2 tablespoons mirin or rice wine

2 tablespoons grated yellow onion

1 tablespoon sesame oil

1 tablespoon black pepper

2 pounds beef rib eye or top sirloin, thinly sliced

4 ounces sweet potato noodles or cellophane noodles, soaked in water to soften

6 shiitake or white mushrooms, sliced

½ (14-ounce) package medium tofu, cut into 1-inch-thick slices

2 scallions, both white and green parts, cut into 5 equal parts, plus more for garnish

1 small carrot, sliced

3 cups beef broth or Korean stock (see Ingredient Tip)

Sesame seeds, for garnish

1. To make the marinade, in a medium bowl, thoroughly combine ½ cup of water, the apple, soy sauce, garlic, sugar, mirin, onion, sesame oil, and pepper.

2. Add the beef, gently massage it with the marinade, and cover the bowl with plastic wrap. Refrigerate for 2 hours to marinate and chill.

3. Put the marinade, beef, and noodles in the Instant Pot.

4. Top with the mushrooms, tofu, scallions, and carrot.

5. Pour in the broth. Lock the lid, and close the steam valve. Set the timer for 10 minutes on High Pressure.

6. When the timer sounds, natural release the steam for 5 minutes, then quick release the remainder. Open the lid, and gently stir. Serve the vegetables, noodles, Bulgogi, and sauce in a shallow bowl.

7. Garnish with chopped scallions and sesame seeds.

INGREDIENT TIP: Korean stock (also known as Korean dashi) is great for this recipe and also to replace water in other recipes. In the Instant Pot, combine 6 cups water, 15 medium dried anchovies (about 1 ounce), and ½ ounce cut dried kelp or kombu. Lock the lid, and close the steam valve. Set the timer for 5 minutes on High Pressure. When the timer sounds, natural release the steam. Strain the solids, and reserve the stock. Discard the solids. Cool down completely before freezing or refrigerating.

Gamja Tang
(Spicy Pork Bone Jumble)

SERVES: 6 | Make Ahead

This rich and hearty dish is packed with savory, umami, and spicy favors. On the stovetop, this soup would be simmering for more than 2 hours, but you'll be able to make a whole pot of this melt-in-your-mouth, tender, juicy pork in a little more than 1 hour here. The Instant Pot pressure cooking keeps all the deep flavors soaked in the pork meat. There is no need to babysit or worry about the liquid becoming too thick and salty.

PREP TIME:
5 minutes

SAUTÉ TIME:
20 minutes

PRESSURE BUILD:
10 minutes

PRESSURE COOK:
2 minutes and 20 minutes

PRESSURE RELEASE:
Quick Release and 10 minutes Natural Release, Quick Release remainder

TOTAL TIME: 1 hour 10 minutes

3 pounds pork neck bones

1 medium yellow onion and quartered

3 tablespoons doenjang (fermented soybean paste)

1½ tablespoons fish sauce

1 tablespoon soy sauce

1 (3-inch) piece ginger, cut into 4 pieces

5 scallions, both white and green parts, cut into 5 equal parts, roots reserved

3 tablespoons gochujang (fermented red pepper paste)

8 garlic cloves, minced

3 tablespoons ground perilla seeds (see Ingredient Tip)

1 teaspoon black pepper, plus more for serving

4 Yukon Gold or russet potatoes, peeled and quartered

6 napa cabbage leaves (optional)

10 perilla leaves, thinly sliced (see Ingredient Tip)

1. Put the pork bones in the Instant Pot. Lock the lid, and close the steam valve. Set the timer for 2 minutes on High Pressure.

2. When the timer sounds, quick release the steam. Open the lid. Drain the pork bones in a colander, and rinse under cold water. Clean the pot.

3. Return the bones to the Instant Pot, and add 5 cups of water, the onion, doenjang, fish sauce, soy sauce, ginger, and scallion roots. Lock the lid, and close the steam valve. Set the timer for 20 minutes on High Pressure.

4. When the timer sounds, natural release the steam for 10 minutes, then quick release the remainder. Open the lid.

5. In a small bowl, combine the gochujang, garlic, perilla seeds, and pepper.

6. Add the gochujang mixture and 8 cups of water to the Instant Pot. Stir well. Press the Sauté button, and set to High. Bring the soup to a boil.

7. After 10 minutes, add the potatoes and cabbage (if using). Cook for about 8 minutes, or until the potatoes soften. Turn off the Instant Pot. Ladle the pork bones, potatoes, and broth into a large bowl.

8. Garnish with perilla leaves and scallions. Add pepper to taste.

PREP TIP: Parboiling the pork bones will release the debris and fat without having to compromise the flavor in this dish. Korean food is all about clean and healthy eating, which is why this step is critical.

INGREDIENT TIP: If perilla seeds are not available, replace them with finely ground sesame seeds. Korean large leeks and chives (or scallions in a pinch) can substitute for the perilla leaves.

6
Poultry and Seafood Dishes

Eomuk Tang | (Korean Fish Cakes and Tofu One-Pot Simmered Dish) 100

Kimchi Godeungeo Jjim | (Braised Spicy Mackerel with Kimchi) 102

Dak Bulgogi | (Chicken Bulgogi) 103

Jogae Jjim | (Seasoned Garlic Clams) 104

Haemul Tang | (Spicy Korean Seafood and Vegetable Mix) 106

Jjimdak | (Braised Chicken with Vegetables and Glass Noodles) 108

Gochujang Chicken Thighs with Rice 110

Samgaetang | (Ginseng Chicken Porridge) 112

Maeun Dalknalgae | (Spicy Sticky Chicken Wings) 114

Dakdoritang | (Braised Spicy Chicken) 116

‹ JOGAE JJIM (SEASONED GARLIC CLAMS), page 104

Eomuk Tang

(Korean Fish Cakes and Tofu One-Pot Simmered Dish)

SERVES: 4 | Make Ahead

Eomuk Tang is perfect for any night when you want to warm up and feel cozy. The fish cakes featured in this dish are premade and can be found in either the freezer or refrigerated aisle of any Asian market. They may be attached to skewers. Because the skewers won't fit in the Instant Pot, simply slide the fish cakes off, and discard the skewers. This is a perfect dish to make ahead; it even tastes better the next day. Serve it with rice and kimchi, if you'd like.

PREP TIME:
10 minutes

PRESSURE BUILD:
10 minutes

PRESSURE COOK:
3 minutes and 5 minutes

PRESSURE RELEASE:
6 minutes Natural Release and 10 minutes Natural Release

TOTAL TIME:
45 minutes

FOR THE BROTH WITH FISHCAKES

8 ounces daikon or Korean radish, peeled and cut into 1-inch dice

6 dried anchovies, heads and guts removed

2 (6-by-6-inch) pieces dried kombu (see Soondubu, Ingredient Tip, page 45)

1 yellow onion, halved

1 (1-pound package) fish cakes (see introduction)

1 (14-ounce) package medium firm tofu, cut into 2-by-4-inch pieces

1 carrot, cut into 1-inch pieces

1 tablespoon soy sauce

1 tablespoon coarse sea salt

1 teaspoon black pepper

1 scallion, both white and green parts, chopped (optional)

1. **To Make the Broth with Fishcakes:** In the Instant Pot, combine the daikon, anchovies, kombu, and onion. Pour in 6 cups of water. Lock the lid, and close the steam valve. Set the timer for 3 minutes on High Pressure.

2. When the timer sounds, natural release the steam for 6 minutes. Open the lid.

3. Using a strainer or chopsticks, discard the anchovies, daikon, and onion.

FOR THE DIPPING SAUCE

⅓ cup soy sauce

1½ teaspoons gochugaru (Korean red chili flakes)

1 teaspoon granulated white sugar

1 garlic clove, minced

1 scallion, both white and green parts, chopped

1 red or green chile pepper, chopped (optional)

1 teaspoon sesame oil

1 teaspoon sesame seeds

4. Add the fish cakes, tofu, carrot, soy sauce, salt, and pepper. Lock the lid, and close the steam valve. Set the timer for 5 minutes on High Pressure.

5. When the timer sounds, natural release the steam for 10 minutes. Open the lid. Ladle the dish into bowls.

6. Garnish with the scallions (if using).

7. **To Make the Dipping Sauce**: In a medium bowl, combine the soy sauce, gochugaru, sugar, garlic, scallion, chile pepper, oil, and sesame seeds. Mix well. Pour into individual-size condiment bowls, and serve with the fish cake soup.

PREP TIP: You can make a whole batch of this broth and use it to replace the water in other soups and stews. It adds a very clean, light, and mild umami flavor to many Korean soups or stews. I like to freeze it in ice cube trays and defrost a couple of cubes in a storage bag in the refrigerator the night before I need them. It will last in the freezer for up to 6 months.

VARIATION TIP: Add fried bean curd and boiled eggs for extra texture. Fried bean curd can be found in any Asian grocery store near the tofu section.

Kimchi Godeungeo Jjim
(Braised Spicy Mackerel with Kimchi)

SERVES: 5 | Super Fast

This recipe is super easy, quick, and perfect to enjoy for a lighter lunch or dinner. Although I particularly enjoy eating this with just rice and drizzling some of the spicy sauce all over it, it does pair well with Gyeran Jjim, or Steamed Eggs (page 18), and Yeongeun Jorim, or Braised Lotus Root (page 20). Cooking this dish in the Instant Pot deepens the taste of the mackerel and kimchi.

PREP TIME:
5 minutes

PRESSURE BUILD:
5 minutes

PRESSURE COOK:
8 minutes

PRESSURE RELEASE:
12 minutes
Natural Release

TOTAL TIME:
30 minutes

1½ cups kimchi (fermented for 1 month or longer)
1 (14.1-ounce) can mackerel (see Ingredient Tip)
1 cup diced (1-inch) daikon
½ yellow onion, sliced
3 tablespoons gochugaru (Korean red chili flakes)

2 tablespoons soy sauce
2 garlic cloves, minced
2 scallions, both white and green parts, chopped
1 teaspoon black pepper
1 jalapeño or green chile pepper, chopped

1. In the Instant Pot, combine the kimchi, mackerel, daikon, onion, gochugaru, soy sauce, garlic, scallions, pepper, and jalapeño. Lock the lid, and close the steam valve. Set the timer for 8 minutes on High Pressure.

2. When the timer sounds, natural release the steam for 12 minutes. Open the lid. Ladle the dish into a big bowl or individual bowls. Serve with rice and side dishes.

INGREDIENT TIP: Canned mackerel can be found at any Korean grocery store (the American version will also work). The fish is preserved in oil, allowing the bones to soften, and it's ready to eat. Be sure to discard the liquid and only use the fish for this recipe. Or use fresh mackerel that can be found at Asian grocery stores. Be sure to gut the fish and cut it into 5 equal parts before cooking.

VARIATION TIP: If you cannot find canned mackerel, try substituting canned tuna for it.

Dak Bulgogi
(Chicken Bulgogi)

SERVES: 5 | Make Ahead

This is a great make-ahead recipe: Prep all the ingredients the night before, and put the marinated meat along with vegetables in a bowl. When you are ready to cook, just pour the ingredients into the Instant Pot, and set the timer.

PREP TIME:
10 minutes, plus 5 hours to overnight to marinate

SAUTÉ TIME:
5 minutes

PRESSURE BUILD:
5 minutes

PRESSURE COOK:
10 minutes

PRESSURE RELEASE:
10 minutes Natural Release

TOTAL TIME:
40 minutes (plus 5 hours to overnight to marinate)

- ¼ cup plus 1 tablespoon soy sauce
- ¼ cup sesame oil
- 3 tablespoons granulated white sugar or brown sugar
- 3 tablespoons minced garlic
- 2 tablespoons honey
- 2 tablespoons rice wine
- 1 tablespoon grated fresh ginger or 1 teaspoon ground ginger
- 1 teaspoon black pepper
- 2 pounds boneless chicken thighs or breasts, cut into 1-by-2-inch chunks
- 1 yellow onion, cut into 1-inch pieces
- 3 garlic cloves, sliced
- 3 scallions, both white and green parts, cut into 2-inch pieces

1. In a large bowl, combine the soy sauce, oil, sugar, minced garlic, honey, rice wine, ginger, and pepper.

2. Add the chicken, and using your hands (you can use gloves), mix to thoroughly combine. Cover the bowl with plastic wrap, and refrigerate for at least 5 hours or up to overnight.

3. Put the chicken and marinade in the Instant Pot. Lock the lid, and close the steam valve. Set the timer for 10 minutes on High Pressure.

4. When the timer sounds, natural release the steam for 10 minutes. Open the lid.

5. Add the onion, sliced garlic, and scallions. Press the Sauté button, and set to High. Cook for about 5 minutes, or until the onion has softened. Turn off the Instant Pot. Ladle the chicken and vegetables onto a big platter. Serve with rice and kimchi.

Jogae Jjim
(Seasoned Garlic Clams)

SERVES: 5

Seafood in Korea is very fresh because Korea is a small peninsula—surrounded by water on three sides. It comes as no surprise then that Koreans eat a lot of seafood—steamed, boiled, raw, sautéed, and fried. It's common to see seafood mixed with spicy peppers, spicy sauces, and fermented or pickled vegetables. This is a traditional dish to make when guests come over or to enjoy at restaurants during family gatherings. But the Instant Pot transforms it into a recipe that is quick and easy to serve any day of the week.

PREP TIME:
10 minutes, plus 3 hours to soak and clean clams

SAUTÉ TIME:
8 minutes

PRESSURE BUILD:
5 minutes

PRESSURE COOK:
1 minute

PRESSURE RELEASE:
5 minutes Natural Release

TOTAL TIME:
30 minutes (plus 3 hours to soak and clean clams)

2 tablespoons canola oil
½ cup chopped kimchi
¼ cup plus 2 tablespoons gochugaru (Korean red chili flakes)
¼ cup sesame oil
3 tablespoons soy sauce
3 tablespoons minced garlic
3 scallions, both white and green parts, chopped
¼ small yellow onion, chopped

2 teaspoons coarse sea salt
1 teaspoon black pepper
1 teaspoon granulated white sugar
4 pounds littleneck clams, scrubbed and cleaned (see Prep Tip)
1 cup water or vegetable broth
Cooked rice, for serving

1. Press the Sauté button, and set to High. In the Instant Pot, combine the canola oil and kimchi. Cook for 5 minutes.

2. Add the gochugaru, sesame oil, soy sauce, garlic, scallions, onion, salt, pepper, and sugar. Mix well, and cook for 3 minutes. Turn off the Sauté mode.

3. Add the clams and water. Lock the lid, and close the steam valve. Set the timer for 1 minute on High Pressure.

4. When the timer sounds, natural release the steam for 5 minutes. Open the lid. Ladle the dish into a big bowl. Serve with rice and any side dishes.

PREP TIP: Clean, scrub, and soak the clams in cold water: Combine 2 tablespoons salt and 4 cups water in a large bowl. Whisk for 30 seconds. Add the clams to the water, and make sure they are all submerged. Soak the clams for a total of 3 hours, carefully removing them, rinsing them, and replacing the water 3 to 4 times during that time. You will see the debris settle on the bottom of the bowl. Salt helps the clams open their mouths and let the dirt out into the water.

VARIATION TIPS: You can add bell peppers and bean sprouts for extra crunch and flavor. Lessen the amount of gochugaru if you prefer the dish to be less spicy.

Haemul Tang
(Spicy Korean Seafood and Vegetable Mix)

SERVES: 5

This dish has an assortment of seafood that is spicy, comforting, and hearty to eat for lunch or dinner. Once reserved for royalty and wealthy families, today's abundance of seafood allows everyone to enjoy this dish. The array of seafood releases deep flavors in the Instant Pot to create a spicy, hearty, yet refreshing meal, perfect served with rice and other sides. Feel free to use any seafood combination you like.

PREP TIME:
15 minutes, plus 3 hours to soak and clean clams and mussels

PRESSURE BUILD:
5 minutes

PRESSURE COOK:
12 minutes

PRESSURE RELEASE:
10 minutes Natural Release

TOTAL TIME:
45 minutes (plus 3 hours to soak and clean clams and mussels)

- 10 to 15 littleneck clams, cleaned (see Jogae Jjim, Prep Tip, page 105)
- 10 mussels, debearded and cleaned (see Jogae Jjim, Prep Tip, page 105)
- 2 fresh or frozen blue crabs, washed thoroughly
- 10 ounces cod or seabass fillet, washed thoroughly and cut into 2-inch pieces
- 10 medium, fresh or frozen, deveined shell-on shrimp, washed thoroughly
- 10 ounces squid or octopus, cleaned (see Prep Tip)
- 2 cups chopped napa cabbage
- 1 yellow onion, cut into bite-size pieces
- 3 scallions, chopped
- 1 cup Korean radish or daikon, peeled and cut into bite-size pieces
- 1 medium carrot, cut into bite-size pieces
- ¼ cup gochugaru (Korean red chili flakes)
- 3 tablespoons minced garlic
- 2 tablespoons tamari (or soy sauce, if gluten is not an issue)
- 1 tablespoon gochujang (fermented red pepper paste)
- 1 tablespoon doenjang (fermented soybean paste)
- 1 teaspoon black pepper

1. While soaking the clams and mussels, separate the top shell of the blue crabs; break and remove the gills. Break the crabs in half.

2. In the Instant Pot, combine the clams, mussels, crab, cod, shrimp, and squid.

3. Arrange the cabbage, onion, scallions, Korean radish, and carrot with the seafood.

4. In a small bowl, combine the gochugaru, garlic, tamari, gochujang, doenjang, and pepper.

5. Pour the mixture all over the seafood and vegetables.

6. Add 6 cups of water. Lock the lid, and close the steam valve. Set the timer for 12 minutes on High Pressure.

7. When the timer sounds, natural release the steam for 10 minutes. Open the lid.

8. Ladle the dish into a big bowl to share family-style. Serve with rice and side dishes.

PREP TIP: To clean the squid, grasp the squid tail in one hand and the head in the other. Carefully hold it firmly, and pull it apart with a slight twisting motion. The head and innards should be discarded. Keep the tentacles and body. Or buy frozen squid, which is ready to eat and available at all Asian markets.

VARIATION TIP: Try adding lobster tails, Dungeness crab (broken into sections), and scallops. To make this extra spicy, add 1 chopped red chile pepper or a jalapeño.

Jjimdak

(Braised Chicken with Vegetables and Glass Noodles)

SERVES: 6 | Make Ahead

My mom used to make this dish a lot when I was growing up; she would serve this along with Yachae Japchae, or Vegetarian Sweet Potato Noodles (page 66). This dish is perfect for meal prepping and to serve bigger crowds. Because Korean cuisine is all about family-style dining, this is a super-popular dish that even pleases the kids, who love the sweetness. This dish works so well in the Instant Pot because all of the aromatics get so deeply cooked into the chicken.

PREP TIME:
5 minutes, plus 1 hour to soak

SAUTÉ TIME:
3 minutes

PRESSURE BUILD:
5 minutes

PRESSURE COOK:
10 minutes

PRESSURE RELEASE:
10 minutes Natural Release

TOTAL TIME:
35 minutes (plus 1 hour to soak)

5 ounces Korean glass noodles, sweet potato noodles, or mung bean noodles
½ cup soy sauce
¼ cup plus 2 tablespoons granulated white sugar
¼ cup minced garlic
¼ cup water or chicken broth
¼ cup mirin or rice wine

¼ cup fish sauce
2 tablespoons honey
1 tablespoon black pepper
4 to 8 dried chile peppers, chopped (optional)
4 pounds bone-in, skin-on chicken legs, thighs, and wings
Sesame seeds, for garnish

1. Put the glass noodles in a large, heatproof bowl, and cover with hot water. Soak for 1 hour. Drain.

2. Meanwhile, to make the sauce, in a medium bowl, combine the soy sauce, sugar, garlic, water, mirin, fish sauce, honey, black pepper, and chile peppers to taste (if using). Mix well.

3. In the Instant Pot, combine the chicken and sauce. Gently mix to coat. Lock the lid, and close the steam valve. Set the timer for 10 minutes on High Pressure.

4. When the timer sounds, natural release the steam for 10 minutes. Open the lid.

5. Press the Sauté button, and set to High. Once the sauce starts to boil, add the soaked noodles. Gently stir, and cook for 2 minutes, or until the sauce has slightly reduced and thickened and the noodles have soaked up much of the liquid. Turn off the Instant Pot. Using tongs, put the chicken and noodles in a big shallow dish.

6. Garnish with sesame seeds.

VARIATION TIP: Feel free to add more vegetables to this dish, like carrots, scallions, shiitake mushrooms, and leeks. After step 4, open the lid, and add the vegetables, set the timer for 3 minutes on High Pressure, and then quick release the steam.

Gochujang Chicken Thighs with Rice

SERVES: 4 | Make Ahead, Super Fast

Serve this one-pot, tasty, spicy chicken and rice recipe along with Gamja Jorim, or Braised Potatoes (page 24), and Yeongeun Jorim, or Braised Lotus Root (page 20). It's a hearty and delicious recipe that also freezes well, so consider doubling the recipe for leftovers or lunches. If you like a thicker sauce, use a cornstarch slurry (see the Prep Tip).

PREP TIME:
5 minutes

PRESSURE BUILD:
5 minutes

PRESSURE COOK:
8 minutes

PRESSURE RELEASE:
10 minutes Natural Release

TOTAL TIME:
30 minutes

2½ cups white short-grain rice

3 tablespoons gochujang (fermented red pepper paste)

2 tablespoons mirin or rice wine

1 tablespoon granulated white sugar

1 tablespoon minced garlic

1 tablespoon tamari

2 teaspoons sesame oil

2 teaspoons sesame seeds, plus more for garnish

1 pound boneless, skinless chicken thighs or breasts

2 scallions, both white and green parts, chopped

1. Rinse the rice several times until the water turns clear.

2. In a bowl or pan that is small enough to fit the inner pot, combine the rice and 2½ cups of water. (A 6-inch cake pan works best.)

3. To make the sauce, in a large bowl, combine ¼ cup of water, the gochujang, mirin, sugar, garlic, tamari, oil, and sesame seeds.

4. Put the chicken and sauce directly into the Instant Pot. Gently mix well.

5. Place the trivet over the chicken, then place the rice bowl on top of the trivet. Lock the lid, and close the steam valve. Set the timer for 8 minutes on High Pressure.

6. When the timer sounds, natural release the steam for 10 minutes. Open the lid.

7. Carefully take the rice and trivet out of the pot. Spoon the rice into individual bowls, and add the chicken on top of the rice.

8. Drizzle with the sauce, and garnish with the scallions and sesame seeds.

PREP TIP: If you'd like to thicken the sauce, turn off the Instant Pot after pressure cooking the chicken and rice, and remove the rice. Press the Sauté button, and set to High. Boil the sauce for 5 to 10 minutes. Add a cornstarch slurry (1 tablespoon cornstarch mixed with 2 tablespoons water), if desired, for a thicker sauce.

VARIATION TIPS: Try adding barley to the rice for added nutrients and taste. Instead of the full 2½ cups rice, use 2 cups short-grain rice and ½ cup barley. Then add 2½ cups water to cook. You also can use chicken legs in place of the thighs or breasts, but you will need to double the cooking time.

Samgaetang
(Ginseng Chicken Porridge)

SERVES: 4 | Gluten Free, Soy Free

In Korea, people love to eat this dish during the hot summer days because they believe in the saying, "Yi yeol chi yeol," which means "fight fire with fire." In other words, eating hot foods will balance their body heat and keep them energized throughout the hot day. This dish has been around for hundreds of years in Korea and was often served to the queen when she felt ill. Samgaetang is my ultimate comfort food during chilly days and when I am feeling under the weather. But you can enjoy it any time of the year with kimchi. Find dried ginseng and jujube (similar to dates) in the rice and grains aisle at your local Korean or Asian grocery store or online.

PREP TIME:
5 minutes, plus 1 hour to soak the rice

PRESSURE BUILD:
5 minutes

PRESSURE COOK:
15 minutes

PRESSURE RELEASE:
10 minutes Natural Release

TOTAL TIME:
35 minutes (plus 1 hour to soak the rice)

3 (1½-pound) Cornish game hens

¾ cup sweet rice, rinsed and soaked in water for 1 hour, divided

10 garlic cloves, peeled and tips removed, divided

3 large dried jujubes, washed, divided

2 dried or fresh ginseng roots (see Ingredient Tip)

2 scallions, both white and green parts, chopped

Coarse sea salt

Black pepper

1. Stuff each Cornish hen cavity with 2 tablespoons of soaked sweet rice, 1 garlic clove, and 1 jujube.

2. In the Instant Pot, combine the hens (belly-side down), 8 cups of water, the remaining sweet rice, remaining 7 garlic cloves, and the ginseng. Lock the lid, and close the steam valve. Set the timer for 15 minutes on High Pressure.

3. When the timer sounds, natural release the steam for 10 minutes. Open the lid. Place each hen in a bowl.

4. Top with the scallions. Add salt and pepper to taste.

INGREDIENT TIP: Ginseng is said to promote stronger cognitive function, increased energy, anti-inflammatory effects, lower blood sugar, fertility, healthy skin, and better sleep, and to prevent flu and reduce stress. Ginseng can be found online or at any health store or Asian grocery store.

Maeun Dalknalgae

(Spicy Sticky Chicken Wings)

SERVES: 4 | Make Ahead

Talk about a fan favorite. This recipe is a true crowd-pleaser, and although it will taste like you have, you actually won't have to spend too much time in the kitchen to make it. The Instant Pot cooks the chicken so quickly, resulting in a moist texture and juicy wing. It's delicious served with a side of Potato Salad (page 26); Jangajji, or Korean Pickled Onion and Jalapeños (page 22); and rice.

PREP TIME:
5 minutes

SAUTÉ TIME:
15 minutes

PRESSURE BUILD:
5 minutes

PRESSURE COOK:
10 minutes

PRESSURE RELEASE:
10 minutes
Natural Release

TOTAL TIME:
45 minutes

1 tablespoon canola oil
3 pounds chicken wings
¼ cup soy sauce
¼ cup granulated white sugar
¼ cup water or chicken broth
2 tablespoons minced garlic
2 tablespoons gochujang (fermented red pepper paste)

2 tablespoons gochugaru (Korean red chili flakes)
2 tablespoons honey
1 tablespoon sesame oil
1 tablespoon sesame seeds, plus more for garnish
1 teaspoon ground ginger
Chopped scallions, for garnish

1. Press the Sauté button, and set to High.

2. Once the screen reads HOT, pour in the canola oil. Add the chicken wings, and sear for about 5 minutes, or until the skin has lightly browned. Turn off the Sauté mode.

3. To make the sauce, in a medium bowl, combine the soy sauce, sugar, water, garlic, gochujang, gochugaru, honey, sesame oil, sesame seeds, and ground ginger.

4. Pour the sauce over the chicken wings. Lock the lid, and close the steam valve. Set the timer for 10 minutes on High Pressure.

5. When the timer sounds, natural release the steam for 10 minutes. Open the lid.

6. Take the chicken out, and set it aside, leaving the sauce in the Instant Pot. Press the Sauté button, and set to High. Let the sauce thicken, stirring, for 8 to 10 minutes. Turn off the Instant Pot.

7. Return the chicken wings to the pot, and coat with the sauce. Serve on a large plate.

8. Garnish with scallions and sesame seeds.

VARIATION TIP: If you want to make this spicier, add more gochujang and some sliced jalapeños. If the sauce is too thin, you can mix 2 tablespoons cornstarch with 2 tablespoons hot water, and add it to the sauce at the end of the sauté.

Dakdoritang

(Braised Spicy Chicken)

SERVES: 6 | Make Ahead

Making this recipe on the stovetop requires lengthy simmering over low heat. Making Dakdoritang using the Instant Pot is not only quick but also allows the flavor to soak in because the flavors aren't evaporating instead. You're guaranteed to end up with a delicious pot of spicy chicken with vegetables that will be the star of your meal. This also makes for great meal prep for the week and is freezer friendly. Serve this with the Gyeran Jjim, or Steamed Eggs (page 18), along with rice and kimchi. Feel free to adjust the spice level by adding less (or more, if you're brave!) gochujang and gochugaru.

PREP TIME:
10 minutes

SAUTÉ TIME:
5 minutes
per batch

PRESSURE BUILD:
5 minutes

PRESSURE COOK:
10 minutes

PRESSURE RELEASE:
10 minutes
Natural
Release

TOTAL TIME:
40 to
50 minutes

1 tablespoon canola oil

3 pounds chicken
legs and thighs

¼ cup soy sauce

¼ cup water or chicken broth

¼ cup gochujang (fermented
red pepper paste)

3 tablespoons gochugaru
(Korean red chili flakes)

3 tablespoons granulated
white sugar

2 tablespoons mirin
or rice wine

1 tablespoon sesame oil,
plus more for garnish

1 teaspoon ground
black pepper

1 teaspoon sesame seeds,
plus more for garnish

8 ounces baby or new
potatoes, halved

3 scallions, both white and
green parts, cut into 2-inch
pieces, plus more for garnish

½ large yellow onion, cut
into 1-inch-thick pieces

1 large carrot, cut into
large chunks

1 jalapeño or red chile pepper,
cut into 1-inch rounds

1 teaspoon minced
fresh ginger

1. Press the Sauté button, and set to High.

2. Once the screen reads HOT, pour in the canola oil. Add as many chicken pieces as will fit in a single layer (don't crowd the pieces), and cook for about 5 minutes, or until seared and light browned in color. Remove the chicken to a plate, and repeat with the remaining chicken pieces. Once it is all seared, return all of the chicken to the Instant Pot. Turn off the Sauté mode.

3. To make the sauce, in a medium bowl, combine the soy sauce, water, gochujang, gochugaru, sugar, mirin, sesame oil, pepper, and sesame seeds.

4. Pour the sauce over the chicken.

5. Add the potatoes, scallions, onion, carrot, jalapeño, and ginger. Lock the lid, and close the steam valve. Set the timer for 10 minutes on High Pressure.

6. When the timer sounds, natural release the steam for 10 minutes. Open the lid.

7. Garnish with scallions, a drizzle of sesame oil, and sesame seeds. Mix gently so everything gets incorporated. Ladle the chicken, vegetables, and sauce into a big bowl.

VARIATION TIPS: You can replace the potatoes with Korean radish or daikon. Cut them into medium chunks. You can also use brown sugar or honey to replace the white sugar.

MEASUREMENT CONVERSIONS

VOLUME EQUIVALENTS	U.S. STANDARD	U.S. STANDARD (OUNCES)	METRIC (APPROXIMATE)
Liquid	2 tablespoons	1 fl. oz.	30 mL
	¼ cup	2 fl. oz.	60 mL
	½ cup	4 fl. oz.	120 mL
	1 cup	8 fl. oz.	240 mL
	1½ cups	12 fl. oz.	355 mL
	2 cups or 1 pint	16 fl. oz.	475 mL
	4 cups or 1 quart	32 fl. oz.	1 L
	1 gallon	128 fl. oz.	4 L
Dry	⅛ teaspoon	—	0.5 mL
	¼ teaspoon	—	1 mL
	½ teaspoon	—	2 mL
	¾ teaspoon	—	4 mL
	1 teaspoon	—	5 mL
	1 tablespoon	—	15 mL
	¼ cup	—	59 mL
	⅓ cup	—	79 mL
	½ cup	—	118 mL
	⅔ cup	—	156 mL
	¾ cup	—	177 mL
	1 cup	—	235 mL
	2 cups or 1 pint	—	475 mL
	3 cups	—	700 mL
	4 cups or 1 quart	—	1 L
	½ gallon	—	2 L
	1 gallon	—	4 L

OVEN TEMPERATURES

FAHRENHEIT	CELSIUS (APPROXIMATE)
250°F	120°C
300°F	150°C
325°F	165°C
350°F	180°C
375°F	190°C
400°F	200°C
425°F	220°C
450°F	230°C

WEIGHT EQUIVALENTS

U.S. STANDARD	METRIC (APPROXIMATE)
½ ounce	15 g
1 ounce	30 g
2 ounces	60 g
4 ounces	115 g
8 ounces	225 g
12 ounces	340 g
16 ounces or 1 pound	455 g

RESOURCES

Many of the Korean ingredients can be found online at Amazon, SayWeee, and Hmart. But watch shipping prices and seasonal price hikes. All the ingredients will be available at your nearest Korean or Asian grocery stores.

Hmart.com

Umamicart.com

Yamibuy.com

ArirangUSA.net

Kimcmarket.com

SeoulMills.com

Gochujar.com

99Ranch.com

SayWeee.com

HanYangMart.com

Amazon.com/korean-grocery/s?k=korean+grocery

Here are some resources to buy the Instant Pot and accessories:

Instant Pot Duo: amzn.to/3kaBKeA

Instant Pot Mesh Steamer: amzn.to/3074kqd

Instant Pot Egg Rack: amzn.to/3H6Qx3V

Instant Pot Sealing Rings: amzn.to/3GXsxjy

Instant Pot Accessory Set: amzn.to/3EP8hi1

INSTANT POT
COOKING CHARTS

The following charts provide approximate times for a variety of foods. To begin, you may want to cook for a minute or two less than the times listed; if necessary, you can always simmer foods for a few minutes to finish cooking.

Keep in mind that these times are for foods partially submerged in water (or broth) or steamed and are for the foods cooked alone. The cooking times for the same foods may vary if additional ingredients or cooking liquids are added or a different release method than the one listed here is used.

For any foods labeled with "natural" release, allow at least 15 minutes natural pressure release before quick releasing any remaining pressure.

Fish and Seafood

All times are for steamed fish and shellfish. Use the trivet to lift the fish/seafood above the cooking liquid so that it steams instead of boils.

	MINUTES UNDER PRESSURE	PRESSURE	RELEASE
CLAMS	2	High	Quick
HALIBUT, FRESH (1-INCH THICK)	3	High	Quick
LARGE SHRIMP, FROZEN	1	Low	Quick
MUSSELS	1	High	Quick
SALMON, FRESH (1-INCH THICK)	5	Low	Quick
TILAPIA OR COD, FRESH	1	Low	Quick
TILAPIA OR COD, FROZEN	3	Low	Quick

Meat

Except as noted, these times are for braised meats—that is, meats that are seared and then pressure cooked while partially submerged in liquid. Unless a shorter release time is indicated, let the meat release naturally for at least 15 minutes, after which any remaining pressure can be quick released.

	MINUTES UNDER PRESSURE	PRESSURE	RELEASE
BEEF, BONE-IN SHORT RIBS	40	High	Natural
BEEF, FLAT IRON STEAK, CUT INTO ½-INCH STRIPS	6	Low	Quick
BEEF, SHOULDER (CHUCK), 2-INCH CHUNKS	20	High	Natural for 10 minutes
BEEF, SHOULDER (CHUCK) ROAST (2 LB.)	35–45	High	Natural
BEEF, SIRLOIN STEAK, ½-INCH STRIPS	3	Low	Quick
LAMB, SHANKS	40	High	Natural
LAMB, SHOULDER, 2-INCH CHUNKS	35	High	Natural
PORK, BACK RIBS (STEAMED)	25	High	Quick
PORK, SHOULDER, 2-INCH CHUNKS	20	High	Quick
PORK, SHOULDER ROAST (2 LB.)	25	High	Natural
PORK, SMOKED SAUSAGE, ½-INCH SLICES	5–10	High	Quick
PORK, SPARE RIBS (STEAMED)	20	High	Quick
PORK, TENDERLOIN	4	Low	Quick

Poultry

Except as noted, these times are for braised poultry—that is, partially submerged in liquid. Unless a shorter release time is indicated, let the poultry release naturally for at least 15 minutes, after which any remaining pressure can be quick released.

	MINUTES UNDER PRESSURE	PRESSURE	RELEASE
CHICKEN BREAST, BONE-IN (STEAMED)	8	Low	Natural for 5 minutes
CHICKEN BREAST, BONELESS (STEAMED)	5	Low	Natural for 8 minutes
CHICKEN THIGH, BONE-IN	10–14	High	Natural for 10 minutes
CHICKEN THIGH, BONELESS	6–8	High	Natural for 10 minutes
CHICKEN THIGH, BONELESS, 1- TO 2-INCH PIECES	5–6	High	Quick
CHICKEN, WHOLE (SEARED ON ALL SIDES)	12–14	Low	Natural for 8 minutes
DUCK QUARTERS, BONE-IN	35	High	Quick
TURKEY BREAST, TENDERLOIN (12 OZ.) (STEAMED)	5	Low	Natural for 8 minutes
TURKEY THIGH, BONE-IN	30	High	Natural

Beans and Legumes

For 1 pound or more of dried beans, use low pressure and increase the cooking time by a minute or two. Unless a shorter release time is indicated, let the beans release naturally for at least 15 minutes, after which any remaining pressure can be quick released. Beans should be soaked in salted water for 8 to 24 hours.

	LIQUID PER 1 CUP OF BEANS	MINUTES UNDER PRESSURE	PRESSURE	RELEASE
BLACK BEANS	2 cups	8	High	Natural
		9	Low	
BLACK-EYED PEAS	2 cups	5	High	Natural for 8 minutes, then quick
BROWN LENTILS (UNSOAKED)	2¼ cups	20	High	Natural for 10 minutes, then quick
CANNELLINI BEANS	2 cups	5	High	Natural
		7	Low	
CHICKPEAS (GARBANZO BEANS)	2 cups	4	High	Natural for 3 minutes, then quick
KIDNEY BEANS	2 cups	5	High	Natural
		7	Low	
LIMA BEANS	2 cups	4	High	Natural for 5 minutes, then quick
		5	Low	
PINTO BEANS	2 cups	8	High	Natural
		10	Low	
RED LENTILS (UNSOAKED)	3 cups	10	High	Natural for 5 minutes, then quick
SOYBEANS, DRIED	2 cups	12	High	Natural
		14	Low	
SOYBEANS, FRESH (EDAMAME, UNSOAKED)	1 cup	1	High	Quick
SPLIT PEAS (UNSOAKED)	3 cups	5 (firm peas) to 8 (soft peas)	High	Natural

Grains

Thoroughly rinse grains before cooking or add a small amount of butter or oil to the cooking liquid to prevent foaming. Unless a shorter release time is indicated, let the grains release naturally for at least 15 minutes, after which any remaining pressure can be quick released.

	LIQUID PER 1 CUP OF GRAIN	MINUTES UNDER PRESSURE	PRESSURE	RELEASE
ARBORIO RICE (FOR RISOTTO)	3–4 cups	6–8	High	Quick
BARLEY, PEARLED	2½ cups	20	High	Natural for 10 minutes, then quick
BROWN RICE, LONG GRAIN	1 cup	22	High	Natural for 10 minutes, then quick
BROWN RICE, MEDIUM GRAIN	1 cup	12	High	Natural
BUCKWHEAT	1¾ cups	2–4	High	Natural
FARRO, PEARLED	2 cups	6–8	High	Natural
FARRO, WHOLE GRAIN	3 cups	22–24	High	Natural
OATS, ROLLED	3 cups	3–4	High	Quick
OATS, STEEL CUT	3 cups	10	High	Natural for 10 minutes, then quick
QUINOA	1 cup	2	High	Natural for 12 minutes, then quick
WHEAT BERRIES	2 cups	30	High	Natural for 10 minutes, then quick
WHITE RICE, LONG GRAIN	1 cup	3	High	Natural
WILD RICE	1¼ cups	22–24	High	Natural

Vegetables

The following cooking times are for steamed vegetables; if the vegetables are submerged in liquid, the times may vary. Green vegetables will be tender-crisp; root vegetables will be soft. Most vegetables require a quick release of pressure to stop the cooking process; for those that indicate a natural release, let the pressure release for at least 15 minutes, after which any remaining pressure can be quick released.

	PREP	MINUTES UNDER PRESSURE	PRESSURE	RELEASE
ACORN SQUASH	Halved	9	High	Quick
ARTICHOKES, LARGE	Whole	15	High	Quick
BEETS	Quartered if large; halved if small	9	High	Natural
BROCCOLI	Cut into florets	1	Low	Quick
BRUSSELS SPROUTS	Halved	2	High	Quick
BUTTERNUT SQUASH	Peeled, ½-inch chunks	8	High	Quick
CABBAGE	Sliced	3–4	High	Quick
CARROTS	½- to 1-inch slices	2	High	Quick
CAULIFLOWER	Whole	6	High	Quick
CAULIFLOWER	Cut into florets	1	Low	Quick
GREEN BEANS	Cut in halves or thirds	3	Low	Quick
POTATOES, LARGE RUSSET (FOR MASHING)	Quartered	8	High	Natural for 8 minutes, then quick
POTATOES, RED	Whole if less than 1½ inches across, halved if larger	4	High	Quick
SPAGHETTI SQUASH	Halved lengthwise	7	High	Quick
SWEET POTATOES	Halved lengthwise	8	High	Natural

INDEX

A

Alliums, 12

Anchovies, dried, 10

Eomuk Tang (Korean Fish
Cakes and Tofu
One-Pot Simmered
Dish), 100–101

Kongbiji Jjigae (Ground
Soybean Stew), 38–39

B

Banchan, 6–7, 11

Beans

Japgokbap (Multigrain
Rice and Beans), 23

Pat Jook (Sweet Red Bean
Porridge), 60–61

Beef, 12

Bulgogi Jungol (Bulgogi
Casserole with
Noodles), 94–95

Galbijjim (Braised Short
Ribs), 90–91

Galbi Tang (Beef Short
Rib Medley), 84–85

Gamja Guk (Egg Drop
Potato Soup), 42–43

Ground Beef Bulgogi
with Rice, 88–89

Jangjorim (Soy-Braised
Beef with Eggs), 86–87

Miyeok Guk (Seaweed
Soup), 52–53

Seogogi Mu Guk (Daikon
Soup), 36–37

Seolleongtang (Milky Beef
Bone Soup), 54–55

Soondubu (Soft Tofu
Stew), 44–45

Tteokguk (Rice Cake
Soup), 46–47

Yachae Gogi Jook
(Beef and Vegetable
Porridge), 74–75

Yookgaejang (Spicy
Shredded Beef
and Vegetable
Chowder), 92–93

Beosot Bap (Mushroom
Rice), 62–63

Beosot Deulkkae Tang
(Mushroom Perilla Seed
Casserole), 68–69

Bossam (Boiled Pork
Belly), 78–79

Braising, 4

Bulgogi

Bulgogi Jungol (Bulgogi
Casserole with
Noodles), 94–95

Dak Bulgogi (Chicken
Bulgogi), 103

Ground Beef Bulgogi
with Rice, 88–89

Jeyuk Bokkeum (Spicy
Pork Bulgogi), 76–77

C

Cabbage, 11. See also Kimchi

Cabbage with Tofu Roll
Casserole, 70–71

Cauliflower, Sweet and Spicy
Gochujang, 28–29

Chicken, 13

Dak Bulgogi (Chicken
Bulgogi), 103

Dakdoritang (Braised Spicy
Chicken), 116–117

Gochujang Chicken Thighs
with Rice, 110–111

Jjimdak (Braised Chicken
with Vegetables and
Glass Noodles), 108–109

Maeun Dalknalgae
(Spicy Sticky Chicken
Wings), 114–115

Samgaetang (Ginseng
Chicken Porridge),
112–113

Clams, Seasoned Garlic
(Jogae Jjim), 104–105

D

Daikon Soup (Seogogi
Mu Guk), 36–37

Dak Bulgogi (Chicken
Bulgogi), 103

Dakdoritang (Braised Spicy
Chicken), 116–117

Dubu Jorim (Spicy
Braised Tofu), 59

Dumplings, Korean (Homemade
Mandu), 32–33

Dwaeji Gogi Gan Jang
Jorim (Soy-Braised
Pork Belly), 82–83

E

Eggplant, Steamed (Gaji
Nameul), 30–31

Eggs

Gamja Guk (Egg Drop
Potato Soup), 42–43

Gyeran Jjim (Steamed
Eggs), 18

Jangjorim (Soy-Braised
Beef with Eggs), 86–87

Eomuk Tang (Korean Fish Cakes
and Tofu
One-Pot Simmered
Dish), 100–101

F

Fish and seafood, 13
Eomuk Tang (Korean Fish
Cakes and Tofu
One-Pot Simmered
Dish), 100–101
Haemul Tang (Spicy Korean
Seafood and Vegetable
Mix), 106–107
Jogae Jjim (Seasoned
Garlic Clams), 104–105
Kimchi Godeungeo Jjim
(Braised Spicy Mackerel
with Kimchi), 102
steaming, 3
Fish sauce, 9

G

Gaji Nameul (Steamed
Eggplant), 30–31
Galbijjim (Braised Short
Ribs), 90–91
Galbi Tang (Beef Short Rib
Medley), 84–85
Gamja Guk (Egg Drop
Potato Soup), 42–43
Gamja Jorim (Braised
Potatoes), 24–25
Gamja Sujebi (Umami
Hand-Torn
Noodles), 64–65
Gamja Tang (Spicy Pork
Bone Jumble), 96–97
Garlic, 11–12
Jogae Jjim (Seasoned
Garlic Clams), 104–105
Ginger, 12
Ginseng Chicken Porridge
(Samgaetang), 112–113

Gluten-free
Beosot Deulkkae Tang
(Mushroom Perilla Seed
Casserole), 68–69
Cabbage with Tofu Roll
Casserole, 70–71
Galbi Tang (Beef Short
Rib Medley), 84–85
Gamja Guk (Egg Drop
Potato Soup), 42–43
Gyeran Jjim (Steamed
Eggs), 18
Hobak Jook (Squash
Porridge), 58
Kkori Gomtang (Oxtail
Soup), 48–49
Miyeok Guk (Seaweed
Soup), 52–53
Pat Jook (Sweet Red Bean
Porridge), 60–61
Potato Salad, 26–27
Samgaetang (Ginseng
Chicken Porridge),
112–113
Seogogi Mu Guk (Daikon
Soup), 36–37
Seolleongtang (Milky Beef
Bone Soup), 54–55
Tteokguk (Rice Cake
Soup), 46–47
Yachae Japchae (Vegetarian
Sweet Potato
Noodles), 66–67
Gochujang, 9
Gochujang Chicken Thighs
with Rice, 110–111
Sweet and Spicy Gochujang
Cauliflower, 28–29
Gyeran Jjim (Steamed Eggs), 18

H

Haemul Tang (Spicy Korean
Seafood and Vegetable
Mix), 106–107

Herbs, 12
High altitude adaptations, 13
Hobak Jook (Squash
Porridge), 58

J

Jalapeños, Korean
Pickled Onion and
(Jangajji), 22
Jangajji (Korean Pickled Onion
and Jalapeños), 22
Jangjorim (Soy-Braised Beef
with Eggs), 86–87
Japgokbap (Multigrain
Rice and Beans), 23
Jeyuk Bokkeum (Spicy Pork
Bulgogi), 76–77
Jjimdak (Braised Chicken with
Vegetables and Glass
Noodles), 108–109
Jogae Jjim (Seasoned Garlic
Clams), 104–105
Joomukbap (Seasoned
Rice Balls), 19

K

Kelp, dried, 10
Kimchi, 7
Kimchi Godeungeo Jjim
(Braised Spicy Mackerel
with Kimchi), 102
Kimchi Jjigae (Kimchi
Stew), 50–51
Kimchi Samgyeopsal Jjim
(Braised Kimchi and
Pork Belly), 40–41
Kongbiji Jjigae (Ground
Soybean Stew), 38–39
Kongbiji Jjigae (Ground
Soybean Stew), 38–39
Korean cuisine
flavors, 5–7
fresh ingredients, 11–13
pantry staples, 8–10

L

Lotus Root, Braised (Yeongeun Jorim), 20–21

M

Mackerel with Kimchi, Braised Spicy (Kimchi Godeungeo Jjim), 102

Maeun Dalknalgae (Spicy Sticky Chicken Wings), 114–115

Maeun Dwaeji Galbi (Sticky Pork Ribs), 80–81

Make ahead
  Bulgogi Jungol (Bulgogi Casserole with Noodles), 94–95
  Dak Bulgogi (Chicken Bulgogi), 103
  Dakdoritang (Braised Spicy Chicken), 116–117
  Dubu Jorim (Spicy Braised Tofu), 59
  Dwaeji Gogi Gan Jang Jorim (Soy-Braised Pork Belly), 82–83
  Eomuk Tang (Korean Fish Cakes and Tofu One-Pot Simmered Dish), 100–101
  Galbi Tang (Beef Short Rib Medley), 84–85
  Gamja Jorim (Braised Potatoes), 24–25
  Gamja Tang (Spicy Pork Bone Jumble), 96–97
  Gochujang Chicken Thighs with Rice, 110–111
  Ground Beef Bulgogi with Rice, 88–89
  Hobak Jook (Squash Porridge), 58
  Jangjorim (Soy-Braised Beef with Eggs), 86–87

Jjimdak (Braised Chicken with Vegetables and Glass Noodles), 108–109

Kimchi Jjigae (Kimchi Stew), 50–51

Kimchi Samgyeopsal Jjim (Braised Kimchi and Pork Belly), 40–41

Kongbiji Jjigae (Ground Soybean Stew), 38–39

Maeun Dalknalgae (Spicy Sticky Chicken Wings), 114–115

Sweet and Spicy Gochujang Cauliflower, 28–29

Yachae Gogi Jook (Beef and Vegetable Porridge), 74–75

Yookgaejang (Spicy Shredded Beef and Vegetable Chowder), 92–93

Mandu, Homemade (Korean Dumplings), 32–33

Mirin, 9

Miyeok Guk (Seaweed Soup), 52–53

Mushrooms, 12
  Beosot Bap (Mushroom Rice), 62–63
  Beosot Deulkkae Tang (Mushroom Perilla Seed Casserole), 68–69

N

Noodles
  Bulgogi Jungol (Bulgogi Casserole with Noodles), 94–95
  Gamja Sujebi (Umami Hand-Torn Noodles), 64–65
  instant pot cooking, 8

Jjimdak (Braised Chicken with Vegetables and Glass Noodles), 108–109

sweet potato, 10

Yachae Japchae (Vegetarian Sweet Potato Noodles), 66–67

O

Onions, 12
  Jangajji (Korean Pickled Onion and Jalapeños), 22

Oxtail Soup (Kkori Gomtang), 48–49

P

Pantry staples, 8–10

Pat Jook (Sweet Red Bean Porridge), 60–61

Perilla Seed Casserole, Mushroom (Beosot Deulkkae Tang), 68–69

Plum syrup, 10

Pork, 13
  Bossam (Boiled Pork Belly), 78–79
  Dwaeji Gogi Gan Jang Jorim (Soy-Braised Pork Belly), 82–83
  Gamja Tang (Spicy Pork Bone Jumble), 96–97
  Homemade Mandu (Korean Dumplings), 32–33
  Jeyuk Bokkeum (Spicy Pork Bulgogi), 76–77
  Kimchi Jjigae (Kimchi Stew), 50–51
  Kimchi Samgyeopsal Jjim (Braised Kimchi and Pork Belly), 40–41
  Kongbiji Jjigae (Ground Soybean Stew), 38–39

Pork (*continued*)

Maeun Dwaeji Galbi (Sticky Pork Ribs), 80–81

Soondubu (Soft Tofu Stew), 44–45

Porridge

Hobak Jook (Squash Porridge), 58

Pat Jook (Sweet Red Bean Porridge), 60–61

Samgaetang (Ginseng Chicken Porridge), 112–113

Yachae Gogi Jook (Beef and Vegetable Porridge), 74–75

Potatoes

Gamja Guk (Egg Drop Potato Soup), 42–43

Gamja Jorim (Braised Potatoes), 24–25

Potato Salad, 26–27

Pot-in-pot insert, 2

R

Recipes, about, 14

Rice

Beosot Bap (Mushroom Rice), 62–63

Gochujang Chicken Thighs with Rice, 110–111

Ground Beef Bulgogi with Rice, 88–89

instant pot cooking, 8

Japgokbap (Multigrain Rice and Beans), 23

Joomukbap (Seasoned Rice Balls), 19

short-grain, 10

Rice Cake Soup (Tteokguk), 46–47

Rice syrup, 10

Rice vinegar, 10

S

Salad, Potato, 26–27

Samgaetang (Ginseng Chicken Porridge), 112–113

Sautéing, 2

Scallions, 12

Seafood. *See* Fish and seafood

Seaweed Soup (Miyeok Guk), 52–53

Seogogi Mu Guk (Daikon Soup), 36–37

Seolleongtang (Milky Beef Bone Soup), 54–55

Sesame seeds, 9

Seweed paper, 10

Simmering, 4–5

Siwonhan mat, 5–6

Soondubu (Soft Tofu Stew), 44–45

Soups and stews

Kimchi Samgyeopsal Jjim (Braised Kimchi and Pork Belly), 40–41

Kkori Gomtang (Oxtail Soup), 48–49

Kongbiji Jjigae (Ground Soybean Stew), 38–39

Miyeok Guk (Seaweed Soup), 52–53

Seogogi Mu Guk (Daikon Soup), 36–37

Seolleongtang (Milky Beef Bone Soup), 54–55

Soondubu (Soft Tofu Stew), 44–45

Tteokguk (Rice Cake Soup), 46–47

Yookgaejang (Spicy Shredded Beef and Vegetable Chowder), 92–93

Soybean Stew, Ground (Kongbiji Jjigae), 38–39

Soy free

Galbi Tang (Beef Short Rib Medley), 84–85

Gyeran Jjim (Steamed Eggs), 18

Hobak Jook (Squash Porridge), 58

Japgokbap (Multigrain Rice and Beans), 23

Kkori Gomtang (Oxtail Soup), 48–49

Pat Jook (Sweet Red Bean Porridge), 60–61

Potato Salad, 26–27

Samgaetang (Ginseng Chicken Porridge), 112–113

Soy sauces, 9

Dwaeji Gogi Gan Jang Jorim (Soy-Braised Pork Belly), 82–83

Jangjorim (Soy-Braised Beef with Eggs), 86–87

Squash Porridge (Hobak Jook), 58

Steaming, 2–3

Stewing, 4

Stocks, 3, 3–4

Super fast

Beosot Deulkkae Tang (Mushroom Perilla Seed Casserole), 68–69

Cabbage with Tofu Roll Casserole, 70–71

Dubu Jorim (Spicy Braised Tofu), 59

Gaji Nameul (Steamed Eggplant), 30–31

Gochujang Chicken Thighs with Rice, 110–111

Gyeran Jjim (Steamed Eggs), 18

Joomukbap (Seasoned Rice Balls), 19

Kimchi Godeungeo Jjim (Braised Spicy Mackerel with Kimchi), 102

Soondubu (Soft Tofu Stew), 44–45

Sweet and Spicy Gochujang Cauliflower, 28–29

Yachae Japchae (Vegetarian Sweet Potato Noodles), 66–67

T

Tofu, 12

Cabbage with Tofu Roll Casserole, 70–71

Dubu Jorim (Spicy Braised Tofu), 59

Eomuk Tang (Korean Fish Cakes and Tofu One-Pot Simmered Dish), 100–101

Soondubu (Soft Tofu Stew), 44–45

Tteokguk (Rice Cake Soup), 46–47

V

Vegan

Beosot Bap (Mushroom Rice), 62–63

Dubu Jorim (Spicy Braised Tofu), 59

Gaji Nameul (Steamed Eggplant), 30–31

Gamja Jorim (Braised Potatoes), 24–25

Hobak Jook (Squash Porridge), 58

Jangajji (Korean Pickled Onion and Jalapeños), 22

Japgokbap (Multigrain Rice and Beans), 23

Pat Jook (Sweet Red Bean Porridge), 60–61

Vegetables. See also specific

Haemul Tang (Spicy Korean Seafood and Vegetable Mix), 106–107

Jjimdak (Braised Chicken with Vegetables and Glass Noodles), 108–109

steaming, 2–3

Yachae Gogi Jook (Beef and Vegetable Porridge), 74–75

Yookgaejang (Spicy Shredded Beef and Vegetable Chowder), 92–93

Vegetarian. See also Vegan

Cabbage with Tofu Roll Casserole, 70–71

Potato Salad, 26–27

Sweet and Spicy Gochujang Cauliflower, 28–29

Yachae Japchae (Vegetarian Sweet Potato Noodles), 66–67

Y

Yachae Gogi Jook (Beef and Vegetable Porridge), 74–75

Yachae Japchae (Vegetarian Sweet Potato Noodles), 66–67

Yeongeun Jorim (Braised Lotus Root), 20–21

Yookgaejang (Spicy Shredded Beef and Vegetable Chowder), 92–93

Acknowledgments

To my mom, who continues to nourish me with a clean and healthy lifestyle and show her love through never-ending nagging, constructive criticism, and acts of service. She has helped take care of my dogs while I spent many hours working on this book and made sure that my coffee mug was always filled to the brim.

To my grandmother, who once raised me as a child and always showed me that food is made with love and dedication. She never took shortcuts and made every-thing from scratch, just like how her grandmother and mother did back in Korea. Her old-school method of Korean cooking is still alive through her daughters and now me, allowing me to share it with all of you.

To my best friend Soo, who first gifted me an Instant Pot back in 2016. I would have never thought to buy a pressure cooker on my own because using it would be too intimidating. I'm glad she kept pushing me to figure it out and start cooking with it because that led to starting up a YouTube channel featuring many of my Instant Pot recipe videos. The Instant Pot is now the most used appliance in my kitchen, next to the espresso machine, of course.

About the Author

CHRISTY LEE graduated from Le Cordon Bleu in 2007. Growing up in Los Angeles, she was fortunate to experience various ethnic foods from restaurants and friends' cooking. Her love of Korean cooking started at a very young age because her grandmother would always be in the kitchen creating delicious recipes. Having a strong mentor, she was able to learn the basics of texture, flavors, and old-school techniques. She currently works as a full-time music teacher in Orange County, and for Shef, an online meal delivery service company, cooking authentic homemade Korean cuisines that are delivered to customers' homes. She is also creator of her own line of sauces called Soy Mayak Sauce, which is also available to purchase through Shef or on Instagram. In her spare time, she manages the social media pages of several restaurants as well as her own YouTube (Christy's Kitchen), TikTok (Missfoodaddict00), and Instagram (@Christy_L_Kitchen), which highlight her cooking journey.

CPSIA information can be obtained
at www.ICGtesting.com
Printed in the USA
JSHW011731260422
25238JS00002B/3